Smuggling
On the Exmoor Coast
1680 – 1850

John Travis

The Exmoor Society

First published 2001 by The Exmoor Society

Copyright © 2001, John Travis

British Library Cataloguing-in-publication Data
A CIP catalogue record for this book is available from the British Library

ISBN   1 899010 60 2

The Exmoor Society
Parish Rooms
Dulverton
Somerset TA22 9DP

Printed and bound in Great Britain by
Hackman Printers Ltd, Rhondda

Contents

List of Maps

List of Illustrations

Acknowledgements

My first thanks must go to the Exmoor Society who invited me to write this book and set me off on what proved to be a fascinating project.

I am extremely grateful to the staff at the Public Record Office, the Westcountry Studies Library and the North Devon Athenaeum for the invaluable help given me while carrying out research. Particular thanks are due to Sue Pullen, Collections Manager at Ilfracombe Museum; Les Franklin, Librarian, and Marjorie Snetzler, Assistant Librarian, at the North Devon Athenaeum; and Dennis Corner, Curator of Dovery Manor Museum, Porlock, for their assistance.

Special mention should be made of Harriet Bridle, who encouraged me to embark on the book and then gave me every support. I am also grateful to Margaret Reed for some helpful pointers when I was beginning my research.

Thanks are due to John Loveless, of Lyndale Photographic, for once again processing my photographs so expertly, and to Bill Pryor and Debbie Clarke for their sterling work with the photocopier.

I owe a particular debt to Lucilla Watson, Andrew Farmer and my daughters Sarah and Emma for reading my manuscript and making constructive suggestions for its improvement. Warm thanks are also due to my daughter Ruth who hurried off to the Public Record Office on several occasions to investigate topics for me.

Most of all, I am very grateful to Gwyneth, my wife, for giving up a substantial part of her school holidays to help me undertake research and take photographs. This book is dedicated to her.

Illustration Acknowledgements

Special thanks are due to the following people and institutions for granting permission to reproduce the following illustrations in this book:

Harriet Bridle: 3, 5, 10, 11, 18, 22, 27, 28; Ned Darch: 30; Dovery Manor Museum, Porlock: 14, 32; Andrew Farmer: 2, 7, 8, 17, 29, 33; Ilfracombe Museum: 1, 4, 6, 12, 13, 15, 19, 20, 24, 25, 26; North Devon Athenaeum: 9, 21; Westcountry Studies Library: 16, 23.

Preface

Smuggling is an 'accursed thing' thundered John Wesley. When the founder of Methodism spoke out in the eighteenth century, contraband-running was rife along the entire length of the British coast and loud were the voices condemning it. The Government constantly reminded the public that smuggling was costing the country massive sums in lost revenue. Members of the establishment denounced the 'pernicious trade' because it openly challenged authority and encouraged a disregard for the law. Merchants protested because they were quite unable to compete on price with those who sold contraband goods. Church leaders denounced smuggling as a great evil because it frequently involved corruption, intimidation and violence.

Not everyone shared these views. Some fishermen and coastal traders claimed they were driven to take up smuggling by need rather than greed, pointing out how hard it was for them to make a living by legal means in an era when their lawful activities were being disrupted by the long wars with France. Many people viewed the smugglers as heroes who defended local autonomy against the might of a distant authority. Others argued that smuggling was an entirely justified response to the crippling duties imposed by an uncaring government. Those actually involved in the trade preferred to be known as 'free-traders' rather than smugglers and claimed to be providing a public service by supplying imported goods such as brandy, tobacco, tea and wine at affordable prices. Certainly the inhabitants of many towns and villages were only too pleased to buy the smugglers' goods and keep their secrets. Even parish priests and country squires sometimes welcomed the opportunity to purchase cheap spirits, wine and tobacco.

This book sets out to tell the story of the long and bitter struggle between the smugglers and the preventive men on the Exmoor coast. The local 'gentlemen of the night' were less vicious and brutal than the smugglers terrorising the coasts of Kent and Sussex, but they were not the swashbuckling heroes that some writers would have us believe. Certainly they were adventurous and daring, but when necessary they used bribery and brutality to achieve their ends. The underpaid and overstretched Revenue officers faced a daunting task in their efforts to stamp out smuggling. Relatively few in number, they were despised and reviled by the tight-knit coastal communities. Today they are often depicted as callous representatives of an uncaring government that would stop at nothing in its efforts to stamp out smuggling. In reality, most were only trying to carry out their duties in the face of overwhelming odds.

Many local histories romanticise smuggling stories and look back with nostalgia to the era when illicit cargoes were run into moonlit coves. This book aims to strip away some of the fanciful myths. The real facts provide a compelling story of a clandestine activity that for over 150 years impacted on the lives of everyone living on or near the Exmoor coast.

Introduction

1 The National Picture

It is perhaps surprising to find that the first reports of smuggling in England concern illegal exports rather than imports. In 1275 an export duty was imposed on raw wool to encourage the home weaving industry, and this prompted some merchants to begin shipping wool to the Continent without paying the new 'custom'. The illegal trade was known as 'owling'. It grew, and in 1614 the Privy Council called attention to the problem, pointing out that it continued 'notwithstanding the many laws and statutes now in force prohibiting the exportation of wool'.

The smuggling of goods into the country was slower to develop. In the sixteenth century duties were first placed on a range of commodities being brought into England and this led to the start of an illegal import trade. After the Glorious Revolution of 1688 brought William III to the throne, smuggling became a much more serious problem. England was drawn into a series of long and expensive wars with France and, to help finance them, crippling import duties were introduced on a whole range of imported

1 Watermouth Cove from Smallmouth Cave, c.1850. Smugglers often used this sheltered cove.

2 Lynmouth, c.1832. The Revenue officers encountered hostility from the inhabitants of coastal villages such as this.

goods such as tea, tobacco, soap and salt. At the same time the Government also introduced a total embargo on French products such as brandy, wine, silk and lace. These measures triggered an explosive growth of smuggling in England, for all of these high-value products were in great demand and the successful landing of a single shipload made massive profits for those who were prepared to take the risk.

New sailing techniques also encouraged illegal imports. Previously all vessels had square sails set across them and needed to have the wind behind them, but in the late seventeenth century ships were developed with the sails set parallel to their keel so that they could take the wind on either side. This was known as 'fore-and-aft rigging'; it enabled vessels to tack into the wind and thus made them much more manoeuvrable. Square-rigged ships had tended to use only ports with good harbour facilities because, to enter,they had to wait for a favourable wind and then had to stay there until the wind changed quarter. The new fore-and-aft-rigged vessels could sail into remote bays, discharge their cargo and leave quickly, regardless of the direction of the wind, and so the risk of them being caught smuggling was much less.

The rapid growth of smuggling in the late seventeenth century prompted the Government to embark on a series of measures to try to limit the damage being done to the economy. The first step was to tackle the old system of 'farming out' the collection of duties to private financiers and merchants, for this had led to serious abuses. In 1671 the Customs service, which collected both import and export duties, was taken out of the hands of these private collectors.

The next stage was to appoint a hierarchy of government officials at each legally recognised port to collect the customs duties and to combat smuggling. In overall charge of the custom-house staff at each port was the collector. Working alongside him was the comptroller, whose principal function was to check that the collector was carrying out his responsibilities properly. The collector and comptroller both signed and sealed all relevant receipts and export documents, and both held keys to the King's warehouse where all seized contraband was stored under their two separate locks. Perhaps the busiest official was the collector's clerk, who had to keep the extremely detailed accounts of all duties collected and salaries paid out. He also had to write all the letters the collector dictated to the Customs Board in London. Another busy official was the land surveyor, who was in charge of the officers actually looking for smuggled goods in the harbours. Working under the land surveyor's supervision were the landwaiters, who went on board all vessels arriving from foreign ports and supervised the landing of their cargoes, the coastwaiters, who did a similar job on coastal vessels arriving from other British ports, and the searchers who checked all goods due to be exported. Tidesmen were stationed on board vessels while they were in port to ensure no goods were smuggled ashore. Tide surveyors went out to vessels at anchor and 'rummaged' their cargoes looking for contraband. Boatmen were also employed. They took Customs officials out in rowing boats to vessels and gave support when a show of strength was needed.

In 1690 the Customs Commissioners appointed the first eight riding officers to patrol the Kent and Sussex coast on horseback, keeping watch for smugglers by day and night. In the years that followed, riding officers were appointed to keep vigil on many other stretches of the English coast and hinterland. They were expected to search for caches of hidden contraband, to listen for rumours and above all to keep a close watch for signs that smuggling runs were about to take place. This was an extremely dangerous job, for, although the riding officer carried a pistol and a cutlass, he was usually alone and at great risk if he came across an armed gang.

The Customs Commissioners soon realised that one of the best ways of tackling smuggling was to intercept vessels before they landed their illicit cargoes. As early as 1680 five Customs vessels were stationed at strategic points along the south and south-east coasts of England. This was a start, but quite insufficient to cope with the rapid upsurge in smuggling. At the end of the century Customs sloops were based at leading ports all round the British coast. In the same period the Excise, which principally levied duties on goods produced or sold within the country, also began to have its own vessels patrolling the coast, because Excise duties had for the first time been imposed on a range of imported goods, including brandy.

Parliament brought in tough legislation to further discourage smuggling. The 1718 Hovering Act stipulated that any ship under 50 tons carrying a cargo of tea, French silks, pepper or brandy that was found hovering (loitering) within 6 miles of the English coast was liable to seizure. An Act of 1721 prescribed transportation for anyone who resisted a Revenue man or who carried arms while smuggling. An Act of 1736 for the first time prescribed the death penalty for the wounding of customs officers. Even an unarmed smuggler resisting arrest now faced transportation. This legislation was called the Act of Indemnity because any smuggler who disclosed the names of other members of his gang was granted a free pardon. It sparked off widespread intimidation and violence, for the smuggling gangs were now even more determined to silence all witnesses. An Act of 1746 was even harsher, prescribing death as the usual punishment for those caught smuggling even if no actual violence was involved. In fact, this draconian penalty was rarely enforced because of strong public sympathy for arrested smugglers. Then in 1784 William Pitt brought in another Hovering Act that authorised the seizure of all ships under 60 tons carrying wine, tea or coffee found within 3 miles of the English coast.

Despite all these measures, the smugglers still had the upper hand. In 1783 a parliamentary committee estimated that contraband running was depriving the Government of at least £2 million in revenue a year at a time when its total annual income was only £12.7 million. So who were these smugglers, where did they operate and what goods did they trade?

Smuggling operations involved men with different talents and from different backgrounds. First there was the financier of the whole operation. He was the 'sleeping partner' who risked his money but not his reputation because he remained anonymous. He might be a respected merchant, a wealthy farmer or even a member of the gentry. The overseas agent was another key figure. It was his responsibility to strike a bargain with the suppliers and to arrange to have the cargo on the foreign quay when the smuggling vessel called to collect it. The master of the smuggling vessel also had a vital part to play. He had to be an expert navigator and know every inch of the coast he was to run the cargo in on, for he had to deliver the contraband to a prearranged place at a prearranged time. His crew likewise needed to be fine seamen, for the smugglers often landed in rough weather, knowing that the revenue vessels were less likely to be at sea then. The 'lander' played the pivotal role on shore. It was his responsibility to plan the landing, hire all the men and horses needed and to ensure that everything ran smoothly. Lookouts would be placed at strategic points to watch for approaching revenue men, while a 'spotsman' would have the responsibility of signalling to the smuggling vessel and guiding it into the landing place. Farm labourers would be hired to act as 'tubmen' and they had to carry two casks, roped together, one across their chest and one on their back. Other men would be employed as 'batmen'; they carried cudgels with which to protect the tubmen against attack.

Smuggling was most prevalent on the south and south-east coasts of England, for these districts had the twin advantages of being within easy reach of sources of supply in France and the Channel Islands and relatively close to London, the principal centre of demand. Nowhere were the gangs more evil and vicious than in Kent and Sussex. Here large gangs terrorised the countryside, tortured informers, fought pitched battles with the Revenue officers and murdered those who opposed them. Suffolk, Essex, Hampshire and Dorset were likewise infested with dangerous bands of ruthless smugglers. South Devon and Cornwall fell into the second rank of smuggling regions, being not too far from supply centres in north-west France and the Channel Islands. Exmoor was at a further remove, as far as the direct traffic across the English Channel was concerned, and this meant that fewer bulk cargoes of contraband were taken there.

Smugglers favoured high-value, luxury goods for which there was a high demand. The volume of smuggling in a particular commodity was subject to sudden swings, rising and falling according to increases or cuts in the rate of duty. For much of the eighteenth century tea was the ideal contraband cargo. This was because legally-sold tea was very expensive, partly because the East India Company had a monopoly on its import and set artificially high prices, but mainly because of high import duties. Massive profits could be made by those who ran tea in illegally, for it could be bought on the Continent for as little as sixpence a pound, but, after being smuggled in, could be sold for as much as five shillings, a price still well below that of legally imported tea. So widespread was the buying of contraband tea that in 1784 the accountant of the East India Company came up with the startling statistic that only one-third of the tea drunk in England was legally imported. Pitt was shocked into action. Later that year he slashed the 119 per cent tax to 12 per cent. That brought a sudden end to tea smuggling!

Wines and spirits were also major contraband cargoes. For much of the eighteenth century large quantities of French wine were illegally imported because it was so heavily taxed. However, in 1784 Pitt also hit this trade hard when he more than halved the import duty. Brandy and gin remained favourite cargoes of the smugglers, for there were massive profits to be made. Brandy could be bought at French ports for as little as five shillings a gallon but the smugglers could sell it in England for five times that price. Gin, or geneva as it was usually called, could be bought at the Dutch distilleries for 2 shillings a gallon and sold in England for four times as much.

Tobacco smuggling likewise offered the opportunity for fat profits. Huge quantities were smuggled in from the Channel Islands and Ostend. It was also unloaded illegally from ships homebound from Virginia and Maryland. In addition the Customs was systematically defrauded when legally imported tobacco was supposedly re-exported from an English port, so that the duty could be reclaimed, only to end up being smuggled in somewhere else along the coast. This type of documentation fraud frequently occurred at Barnstaple and Bideford on the North Devon coast.

In the eighteenth century the preventive forces had little success in their efforts to curb smuggling. At sea the Customs vessels usually encountered swifter and more heavily armed smuggling vessels. On land the riding officers were few in number and inadequately trained, and had to cope with the hostility of the communities they policed. Some riding officers were undoubtedly in league with the smugglers on whom they were supposed to be spying and those who tried to do their job loyally were quite unable to deal single-handed with large gangs. In fact, corruption was rife throughout the prevention service because the officers were poorly paid and the smugglers could afford to offer big bribes.

Another problem bedevilling the preventive forces was the intense rivalry between the different branches of the service. The port officials and riding officers were intensely jealous of the crews of the Revenue cutters, who made far more seizures than they did and thus were entitled to more prize money. On the other hand the commanders of the Revenue cruisers,

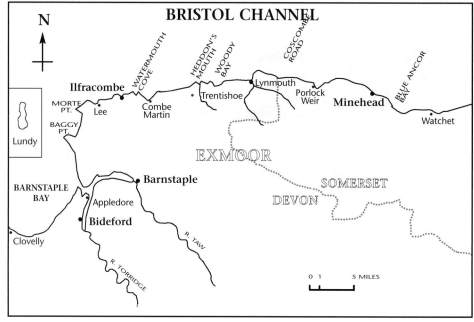

Map 1   Exmoor and adjacent areas.

fiercely independent to a man, hated the fact they were supposed to take their orders from land-based Customs collectors and often ignored their instructions when out at sea. Meanwhile on land the riding officers resented the fact they received little assistance from either the port officials or the Revenue cutters, but instead had to patrol their beat alone.

In the first part of the nineteenth century, the Government introduced measures that at last began to improve the efficiency and morale of the Revenue men. First, in July 1810 the Preventive Waterguard was formed. This new force was intended to form a link between the riding officers on land and the Revenue cutters out at sea. The Preventive Waterguard were provided with small rowing galleys and it was their job to patrol bays and inshore waters that the Revenue cutters could not easily reach. Then in January 1822 the Revenue cutters, riding officers and Preventive Waterguard were completely amalgamated into a new force to be known as the Coast Guard (these two words soon becoming one). Naval training techniques were introduced, seamanship was improved, discipline was tightened up and soon the new integrated service began to score dramatic successes in the war against the smugglers.

3   The entrance to Combe Martin Bay, 1813. To the east, the towering cliffs of Great Hangman provided a formidable barrier to the interior.

Other measures to improve the efficiency of the Coastguard service followed. Officers were removed from their home area and set down in distant parts of the country where they would have no local loyalties and would be less susceptible to bribery and intimidation. Coastguard cottages were built in many coastal villages to accommodate these men. The Coastguard service also began to pay more attention to intelligence-gathering. Paid informers in foreign ports began to send back detailed reports listing the names of vessels loading contraband, their masters, homeports and cargoes. This meant that the Revenue cutters had advance warning of a likely run and were able to lie in wait for the smuggling vessels.

These measures turned the tide of battle and by the 1840s most smugglers had given up the unequal struggle. A complete change of Government economic policy then delivered the final hammer blow. As early as the 1770s Adam Smith had advocated a free trade policy as the only effective answer to smuggling and belatedly the Government came to share this view. Between 1842 and 1845 duty was completely removed on no less than 1,200 items. In 1860 the Treaty of Commerce with France led to the abolition of many of the remaining duties. The result was that smuggling became confined to just a few articles still subject to duties, notably tobacco and spirits.

In 1857 the Customs Board reported that 'smuggling had greatly diminished'. It attributed this to the reduction in duties and the fact that the smuggler was 'no longer an object of general sympathy or a hero of romance'. Yet, while it was true that the introduction of free trade had hit smuggling hard, there does not seem to be a shred of evidence to suggest that local people had withdrawn their support for the smugglers. What had changed was that the economic justification for smuggling had gone and the Government was bearing down on the contraband runners with more integrated and efficient forces.

The great days of smuggling had come to an end. In 1864 the Customs Commissioners were able to announce for the first time that not a single organised smuggling run had been reported to them in the previous year. They claimed contraband running by this time was confined solely to the concealment of small quantities of tobacco and spirits on board regular trading vessels. The traditional smugglers had finally been vanquished.

2 The Exmoor Coast

Before surveying smuggling on the Exmoor coast, it is important to define the geographical limits of the region and to provide some background information about the physical, social and economic environment in which the early smugglers were operating. Only then will it be possible to understand the opportunities and obstacles facing the contraband runner on this section of the English seaboard.

For the purposes of this book, the Exmoor coast will be considered as extending from Morte Point in the west to Blue Anchor Bay in the east (see Map 1), although some reference will also be made to Barnstaple Bay because the port of Barnstaple handled much of Exmoor's trade. In Barnstaple Bay the waters of the Taw and Torridge mingle and flow out to sea over a sandbar known as the Bar. The jagged reefs and stacks of Morte Point mark the northern limit of the huge bay and the start of the Exmoor region. Here the seacoast turns to run eastwards and at once takes on a different character; high hog's-back cliffs and a boulder-strewn foreshore replacing the dunes, sandy beaches and estuarine mudflats of Barnstaple Bay. This 20-mile stretch of coast ranks among the most inhospitable in England. Not until Minehead is reached do the cliffs and rocky foreshore finally come to an end, to be replaced by the lowlands and sandy beaches fringing Blue Anchor Bay.

On first inspection, this bleak and forbidding coast might have seemed quite unsuitable for smuggling. The Bristol Channel's strong tidal currents made inshore navigation difficult, rocky shorelines made landings hazardous and high cliffs presented a formidable barrier to the interior. Once inland the smuggler would have been faced with still more problems, for the upland terrain and scarcity of roads meant that in the eighteenth century much of the interior was still impassable by wheeled vehicle.

Yet some of these apparent disadvantages were in fact advantages for the determined smuggler. The strong tidal currents and rocky shorelines held no fears for local mariners accustomed to navigating these inshore waters, but may have persuaded some preventive crews, who were less familiar with the coast, to keep their vessels well out to sea. The hog's-back cliffs likewise could be seen as an advantage during a landing. They become steeper lower down and this meant that the shore could not easily be seen from the clifftop. The wild terrain also favoured the smuggler, for in the eighteenth century the Customs Board did not think it practical to have riding officers patrolling such a remote and inaccessible coast. What is more, the lack of roads meant that revenue officers could not be suddenly rushed in if it was suspected that a landing was about to take place in a remote bay.

Ilfracombe was the principal port on the Exmoor coast. This little town was a harbour of refuge for ships seeking shelter from westerly gales. In 1790 John Savage was on one such vessel forced into Ilfracombe by a storm. He described a port with a flourishing coastal trade: 'They have near 100 sail of freighting sloops and brigs at this place, whose chief employ is fetching coal from Wales for this and many other ports.' Ilfracombe also had another function, providing pilots to guide Bristol-bound ships up the Bristol Channel. The port was of sufficient importance to warrant it having its own Customs collector, with jurisdiction over the coast from Morte Point in the west to the county border with Somerset in the east.

Minehead was the only other port of consequence on the Exmoor coast. Daniel Defoe wrote of it in 1722: 'No ship is so big but that it may come in, and no weather so bad but the ships are safe when they are in.' Minehead at this time was inhabited by rich merchants, trading mainly with Ireland, but also with Virginia, the West Indies and the Mediterranean. Locally made woollen goods had long been the leading export, while tobacco was a principal import. Like Ilfracombe, it was an officially designated port with its own collector and custom-house. Minehead's overseas trade went into steep decline in the late eighteenth century and by 1830 it had only some six

4 Combe Martin in 1811. Smugglers used pack animals such as these to carry contraband inland from Exmoor harbours and coves. Note the limekiln.

vessels, trading mainly with South Wales and Bristol. Four years later, Minehead lost its status as a registry port and was placed under the jurisdiction of the collector of the port of Bridgwater.

Just to the west of the Exmoor coast were two much more important ports. Barnstaple, on the Taw, and Bideford, on the Torridge, were great rivals. For centuries their merchants had prospered, sending out sailing ships to trade with the Continent, Ireland and the American colonies. Locally made cloth and pottery had been two of the principal exports, while dried cod from Newfoundland and tobacco from Virginia and Maryland had been two of the main return cargoes. Although only 8 miles apart, the trade of the two rival ports was sufficient to warrant both having a collector and supporting officials.

Lynmouth was a small Exmoor fishing village under the jurisdiction of the Ilfracombe Customs collector. Its tidal harbour never had a significant foreign trade, but was home to two or three coastal trading vessels, mainly visiting Wales to fetch limestone for the limekilns and coal for heating, but also making occasional trips to Bristol for supplies. Lynmouth was also an important centre of the herring fishery.

Porlock likewise had a tidal harbour at Porlock Weir, this being controlled by the Minehead Customs collector. In 1682 William Culliforde, Surveyor-General of Customs, visited it and found 'a good harbour for small vessels, to which place there are several that belong, which trade overseas'. Porlock was soon to lose this foreign trade to Bristol. Like Lynmouth, it had an important herring fishery. Culliforde described how every summer 'a great concourse of people and small craft' gathered there and 'great quantities of herrings' were taken and cured.

At Watchet there was another harbour under the jurisdiction of the Minehead Customs collector. By the late seventeenth century it was fast becoming a serious rival to its parent port. William Culliforde wrote of it in 1682: 'From being beggars, within this last 10 years the whole town is grown exceeding rich and have now as great an overseas trade as Minehead.' Watchet's prosperity was short-lived. Its foreign trade collapsed as quickly as it had grown up and by 1797 its only trade was said to be the shipment of kelp to other Bristol Channel ports.

Apart from these ports and harbours, there were only a few small bays and coves on the bleak Exmoor coast where contraband might be run in. Lee Bay, three miles west of Ilfracombe, provided one break in the cliffs and

5 Limekiln at Heddon's Mouth, 1908. In earlier times, coasting vessels bringing limestone to the kiln sometimes had contraband concealed under their legitimate cargo.

was much frequented by smugglers, because it afforded the shelter needed for the landing of contraband. Two miles east of Ilfracombe, the long inlet of Watermouth Cove afforded another gap in the cliffs. Here by day coasters brought limestone from Wales to be fired in a kiln, while after dark other small vessels sometimes ran in illegal cargoes.

Combe Martin lies in a much wider bay, but one disparaged by Thomas Westcote in 1630 as 'a poor haven'. Pulled up on the beach here might be seen a few small sailing vessels that had brought in coal, or limestone for the beachside limekilns. Combe Martin had neither quay nor mooring place and this may be the reason why there is little documentary evidence of it being used by smugglers. John Savage was certainly not impressed when he went there in 1790. He described it as:

> A long straggling village, the vilest and dirtiest I ever saw, the heaps of dung that lie in the streets pretty frequent, thrown out from stables and cowhouses, give no pleasure to ye eyes or nose. The scrubby cottages and poor public houses are but a kind of standing dunghills, and some of the nasty women I saw in them look like moving ones, so that I think it might properly be called the village of dunghills.

East of Combe Martin rise up the massive cliffs of Great Hangman and Holdstone Down. This rocky coast provides magnificent scenery but very few coves where smugglers might operate. Not until Heddon's Mouth is there a break in the cliffs. Here stood a limekiln, proof that trading vessels could come up on the beach there, though smugglers may have preferred to anchor offshore and bring the cargo ashore in smaller boats. Two miles further east lies Woody Bay, where there was another limekiln. Smugglers also used this remote cove, which was far from the nearest road and hidden away under towering cliffs.

East of Woody Bay was another Lee Bay. Here too was a limekiln, indicating that it was occasionally visited by coasting vessels, but the only evidence that smuggling once went on there comes in William Riddell's *Guide to Lynton and Lynmouth*, c.1885. This little guidebook states that in about 1860 workmen demolishing an old cottage found that the back of a bedroom cupboard was formed by a large stone, that on removal led to a shaft. This led down to a cellar deep underground, which the excited labourers found to be empty. It was supposed to have been used by a well-known smuggler called Fence.

Having considered the locations where contraband runs took place, it is

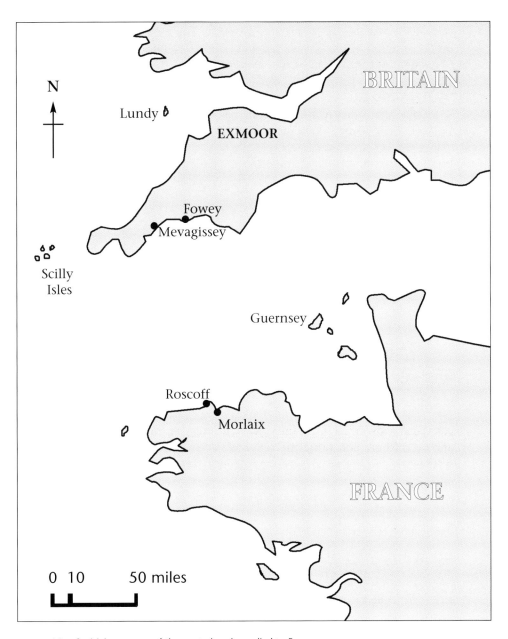

N

Lundy

BRITAIN

EXMOOR

Fowey
Mevagissey

Scilly
Isles

Guernsey

Roscoff
Morlaix

FRANCE

0 10   50 miles

Map 2   Major sources of the contraband supplied to Exmoor.

6 Shipbuilding at Ilfracombe, c.1830. This was a long-established industry at several harbours on the Exmoor coast.

important to look at the economic activities from which the majority of smugglers were recruited. The traditional maritime occupations gave men just the skills needed to become proficient smugglers. What is more, their legitimate activities provided a perfect cover for the running of illicit cargoes.

Herring fishing had long been a mainstay of the economy at Ilfracombe, Lynmouth, Combe Martin, Porlock and Minehead. Millions were caught from open boats, but large numbers were also caught in huge fish traps known as weirs, which were constructed of stakes interwoven with wattles and set round large pools on the shore. Many of the fish were wood-smoked to produce 'red herrings' in what were known as 'red houses', but large numbers were also salted to produce 'white herrings'. The cured herring were then packed in barrels and most were sent to Bristol for export to the Mediterranean and West Indies. In 1797, however, the era of huge catches finally came to an end and the local fishermen were obliged to find other ways of supplementing their living. They were skilled seamen and had an intimate knowledge of the inshore waters, so it is hardly surprising that some chose to work for the smugglers.

The Ilfracombe pilots were much involved in small-scale smuggling.

They had a legitimate reason to meet all the ships entering the Bristol Channel, for it was their job to guide them to Bristol or one of the other ports. Consider the unique opportunities they had for illegal trading. They had to meet ships loaded with tobacco from Virginia and Maryland, vessels from the West Indies carrying rum, and others from Europe laden with brandy and wine. The captains and crew of many of these ships welcomed the opportunity to do some illegal trading on their own account. Having bought contraband, the Ilfracombe pilots were well equipped to land it, for they had an unrivalled knowledge of the local coast.

Coasting vessels operating from the Exmoor ports and harbours also had every opportunity to engage in small-scale smuggling. Little colliers regularly shipped in Welsh coal. Coasters brought limestone across from Wales and the lime produced in the many Exmoor kilns was used to neutralise the acid moorland soil. Other sailing vessels went regularly to Bristol, to collect groceries and other essential goods. Any of these vessels, could, if their master wished, be diverted to Lundy to pick up a cargo of smuggled wine, spirits or tobacco, or could rendezvous in the Bristol Channel with a ship inward bound for Bristol to pick up some duty-free goods. This contraband could then be concealed under a legitimate cargo and landed on the Exmoor coast. Usually the amounts landed on each trip were quite small: a few kegs of brandy or geneva, a few packets of tea or tobacco, perhaps a dozen bottles of wine. Yet, over a period of time, the quantities mounted up, and such imports were difficult to detect.

So just how serious a problem was smuggling on the Exmoor coast? The Customs records for the region list seizures that are modest when compared with those made on many sections of the south coast of England, and this tends to give the impression the problem was much less serious on the Exmoor coast. This may well have been the case, for the sea trip from the main sources of supply in France and the Channel Islands was much longer (see Map 2). The greater risk of smuggling vessels being intercepted by Revenue cutters while making the long sea journey round Land's End and along the Atlantic coast of Cornwall must have deterred some smugglers.

There is, however, another possible explanation for there being fewer records of contraband seizures on the Exmoor coast. Smugglers would have been much more difficult to catch in this wild and inaccessible area and there were far fewer Revenue men employed than in many other English coastal districts. So the fact that smugglers were not often detected in the Exmoor region does not in itself prove that they were less active there.

It does seem that in the summer months the majority of smugglers preferred to make the shorter sea journey from France or the Channel Islands to the coast of North Cornwall and then to move their contraband up country by land. In winter, though, it was dangerous to land cargoes on the exposed North Cornwall coast and the evidence suggests that at that time of the year most smugglers preferred to discharge their contraband in the more sheltered bays and coves along the Exmoor coast.

Smuggling on Exmoor – there can be few more difficult subjects to research! The first problem is that smuggling is by nature a secretive activity, so digging out information is a challenging task. Reports of smugglers are found only when they are caught and, as already explained, on the Exmoor coast this occurred only rarely. The second difficulty is that the region was remote and cut off from the main centres of population, so events there received little coverage in the regional newspapers. There is, however, one excellent source available in the Customs records kept at the Public Record Office. Letter-books containing transcripts of letters written by the Customs collector at Barnstaple to the Customs Board in London have survived for the period from 1743 and from the Board to the Barnstaple collector from 1717 onwards. For Ilfracombe, copies of the letters from the collector to the Board still exist for the period from 1778 as do those from the Board to the collector written from 1792 onwards. Unfortunately, for Minehead only the transcripts of the letters written from the collector to the Board between 1833 and 1835 have survived and this means that there is less information available for the east of the region. These collector's letter-books, together with a report made by William Culliforde, Surveyor-General of Customs, in 1682, form the main primary records on which this account is based, although contemporary accounts from local newspapers have been used to fill out the picture whenever a relevant account has been found.

The scarcity of records makes it difficult to form a definitive view of smuggling on the Exmoor coast. It is rather like trying to construct a jigsaw for which many of the pieces are missing. All one can do is to assemble those fragments of evidence that still exist and piece together the best picture possible. What follows is a chronological account of smuggling in the region, interspersed with chapters focusing on characters and events to highlight particular aspects of the activities of the smugglers and the work of the preventive men. Chapter 1 begins by considering a series of early smuggling incidents at Minehead.

1

Corruption at Minehead

In June 1682 William Culliforde, Charles II's Surveyor-General of Customs, arrived in Minehead to inspect the port. Reports that smuggling was taking place openly and blatantly at some south-western ports had prompted the Customs Board to send its Surveyor-General to investigate. On reaching Minehead, Culliforde went straight to the custom-house and began taking evidence from informants. His subsequent report was an astounding catalogue of contraband running, corruption, violence and intimidation in what was then a busy port.

John Fry, a stonemason, gave evidence that at Christmas 1681 a ship called the *Swallow* had berthed in Minehead harbour. Once it was dark he had seen men secretly begin to unload part of her cargo of wine and brandy. Thirty hogsheads were carried to the cellar of Thomas Wilson, a merchant and one of the owners of the vessel. Over the next four nights, a wagon belonging to a Mr Hooker of Taunton had come several times to carry the brandy and wine away. Fry stated that on one occasion James Hellier and Henry Clement, two Minehead tidesmen, had actually stood and watched the loading of the wagon. Even more disturbing was the fact that Elias Blake, the local constable, had been one of the men employed to move contraband out of the ship.

Fry said that three weeks later he had been hired by Richard Sandys, the Minehead Customs collector, to board the ship *Mayflower*, newly arrived with a cargo of salt, wine and brandy, and stay there all night to ensure that no part of the cargo was illegally removed. Also on the vessel, supposedly on guard, were James Hellier and Henry Clement. All through the night these tidesmen had verbally abused Fry, presumably because he had previously spied on the smugglers while they were unloading wine and brandy from the *Swallow* and was now preventing contraband being removed from the *Mayflower*. Hellier had left the ship early in the morning and when, a little later, Fry had gone onto the quay he had been at once attacked by a Mr Wheeler, master of the *Swallow*, and several other assailants. In his statement Fry claimed they 'very much beat him and wounded him, by breaking his head and bruising his body, so that this informant spit and

7 Minehead in 1863. When William Culliforde visited the port in 1682, he found a busy harbour where Customs officials turned a blind-eye to smuggling.

voided much blood for above nine days and was in great danger of death, the said assailants being armed with clubs and staves'.

Fry confessed that the previous September he himself had helped the smugglers. He had been paid 4s. 6d to work with four other men at night hoisting hogsheads of wine and casks of brandy out of the *Merchant's Adventure*, and then to carry the contraband into the house of Thomas Wilson, the merchant, on the quay. James Hellier had watched this taking place and had done nothing to prevent it.

Daniel Yates, another tidesman, gave evidence that in June 1679 the ship *Increase* had arrived from Virginia loaded with tobacco. He said that the same night James Hellier and John Bennet, another tidesman, had been present while 5,000 lbs. of tobacco were smuggled ashore. Hellier and Bennet had been paid 40 shillings apiece by Mr Danter, the master of the ship, for allowing the Revenue to be defrauded in this way.

Yates confessed that, once, he himself had turned a blind eye to smuggling. He and Hellier had been appointed to search a vessel from Ireland that entered the harbour, supposedly just carrying ballast. The two of them had found 864 gallons of brandy and wine hidden under the bal-

8 Watchet in 1811. In 1682 William Culliforde had discovered that smuggling was rife here.

last, but had not reported this to the collector. Later this brandy and wine had been smuggled ashore and the master of the ship had paid the two tidesmen a golden guinea each.

Peter Bond, a shoemaker, presented even more shocking evidence. He claimed that practically all the Customs officers at Minehead were involved in the smuggling. Bond said that he had lived in a house on the quay for three years and during that time he had often seen hogsheads of wine, casks of brandy and rolls of Irish frieze smuggled ashore from ships under cover of darkness. Sometimes James Hellier and Henry Clement had stood and watched this happening. The shoemaker claimed it was 'a general practice and custom in the night time to have great quantities of all sorts of goods run by the town porters and seamen, which was not possible to be done without the privy and consent of all or most of the officers in the town'.

Bond particularly instanced an occasion in December 1680 when a ship inward bound for Bristol had called at the harbour and James Hellier had gone on board as tidesman. That night Bond had seen about 40 packs of cloth unloaded from the vessel by porters and carried to the back wall of Thomas Wilson's house; from there it was lifted up by ropes into his court-yard. The work had gone on until it was almost light. That morning he had gone and informed George Blake, a landwaiter, and William Hayman, the searcher. They had pretended to go and search the house but had claimed they could find nothing.

Bond also stated that in 1681 the smugglers had accused him of spying on them. Richard Start, a merchant, had gone to Colonel Luttrell, the owner of Dunster Castle and a Justice of the Peace, and had obtained a warrant to have him thrown into prison. After three days Bond had been brought before Justice Luttrell. The only charge Start had laid against Bond was that he was 'a nightwalker' and that this had prevented the merchants doing 'their business'. Start had requested that Bond 'might be whipped publicly in their town for a warning to other rogues'. Colonel Luttrell had agreed to the request and Bond was sent back to gaol to await the sentence being carried out. Finding that there was no one in Minehead prepared to administer the whipping, Luttrell had sent one of his domestic servants from Dunster Castle to do the job. On market day Bond had been 'hand bolted with iron shackles' and 'publicly whipped through the town', receiving more than 100 lashes.

This is a remarkable example of the local squire actually encouraging smugglers and punishing a man who dared to speak out against them. In his report Culliforde commented: 'You will see what influence Colonel Luttrell has upon the town or rather the town upon him.' The evidence suggests this gentleman was doing all that he could to obstruct the Surveyor-General's attempts to investigate smuggling at the port.

So what was the outcome of the Surveyor-General's inspection of Minehead? Henry Clement was dismissed from the King's service, so a promise made by Colonel Luttrell to protect him against dismissal came to nothing. James Hellier, a tidesman whom Culliforde described as 'a very cunning fellow' who had 'ruled and governed the port for many years much to His Majesty's prejudice', was likewise sacked. The Customs collector and comptroller both seem very lucky to have kept their positions, for they must have been either grossly incompetent not to have realised what was going on, or in league with the smugglers.

William Culliforde also went to inspect nearby Watchet. When he arrived, Francis Vickery, a mariner, told him that earlier that year a ship called the *Devonshire* had come into the harbour. Out of this vessel 200 packets of linen and a large quantity of wine had been smuggled ashore at night-time. It had taken 20 men and boys six hours to carry the contraband ashore; some had been taken into an alehouse and some into a private house. Robert Dashwood had been the landwaiter in charge at Watchet, but he had simply watched from the quay and later from the vessel, and had made no effort to prevent the run.

Decisive action was taken. Robert Dashwood was sacked. Culliforde declared that this landwaiter's 'knavery' had effectively made Watchet a free port where no customs duties were paid and as a result its overseas trade had grown to the extent that it rivalled Minehead. Culliforde recommended that in future 'no goods whatsoever except coals be suffered to be landed at Watchet, as was never permitted till of late years'. Instead vessels would have first to call at Minehead, pay Customs duties and only then be given a permit to go on to Watchet. The merchants were furious!

2

Smuggling in the Early Eighteenth Century

It is particularly difficult to reconstruct the pattern of smuggling on the Exmoor coast in the first half of the eighteenth century. The problem is that the Barnstaple letter-books are almost the only source for the period. Letters from the Customs Board to the Barnstaple collector have survived from 1717 and from the collector to the Board from 1743. Yet within these records sufficient information exists to show that smugglers were active on the Exmoor coast at this time.

The first relevant record is found in July 1718, when the Customs Board sent a letter to the Barnstaple collector, and presumably to his colleagues at Ilfracombe and Minehead, warning that French smuggling vessels were lurking off the coast. The message stated:

> It appears some French vessels are hovering on your coast where they lye for opportunity to put their brandy into vessels which are employed in carrying limestones to your and other ports. And you are to cause all such vessels to be diligently searched.

With this message was enclosed a copy of a letter that the collector at Swansea had sent the Board. It stated that recently there had been seen 'between Clovelly Roads and the island of Lundy two French ships laden with wine and brandy and other goods'. It went on to claim that French smuggling ships were 'constantly' venturing into the Bristol Channel and waiting there to rendezvous with the vessels which in the summer months were engaged in carrying limestone to Barnstaple and Bideford, together with 'Ilfracombe and that part of the coast'. The masters of the local coasting vessels returning with cargoes of limestone from Wales must have known where to meet up with French smuggling vessels. After haggling over the price of contraband, they would have sailed into Exmoor harbours and creeks with smuggled goods hidden under their limestone.

Further proof of the involvement of limestone vessels in the smuggling trade came in July 1722. The Swansea collector advised the Customs Board

9 Vessels at Barnstaple Quay, 1842. The building on the far right was at one time the custom-house.

that the *Neptune* of Bideford, John Lancey master, and two other unknown smuggling ships, were hovering in the Bristol Channel with wine and brandy from France on board, waiting to meet limestone coasters. The Swansea collector wrote: 'A great clandestine trade is carried on in that Channel between the smuggling vessels and the vessels employed in carrying limestone from that part of Wales into Devonshire.'

Very few records of seizures on the Exmoor coast exist for this early period, but this seems to be the result of failings in the preventive system, rather than a lack of contraband landings. The above reports of smuggling vessels operating in the Bristol Channel show that illicit cargoes were being run in and it seems the Customs authorities were powerless to stop them. It is significant that the only two recorded seizures were at harbours under the direct supervision of collectors, where there was at least a skeleton staff of Customs officers. Four gallons of wine were seized at Ilfracombe in January 1724 and six gallons of wine at Minehead in July 1728.

The total lack of seizures on the remoter parts of the Exmoor coast is hardly surprising, given the poor policing. Not a single riding officer was stationed in the region at this time, while Revenue vessels patrolled only spasmodically. In 1720 the Admiralty smack *Thomas and Mary* was ordered to cruise between Kingroad in the port of Bristol and Bideford 'to hinder the running of goods'. Other Revenue vessels occasionally operated in the Bristol Channel for short periods in the 1720s, but in the two decades after that. Exmoor smugglers were free to carry on their work without interruption.

The local collectors lacked the resources needed to tackle the contraband runners, but this did not prevent the Customs Board becoming irritated that their officials seemed unaware of smuggling going on almost 'under their noses'. In September 1734 the Board sent the local collectors details of a smuggler who was running contraband into the region. It stated:

> One Richard Robinson, a notorious smuggler who lives at Guernsey, carries on a considerable clandestine trade by exporting from that place tea, brandy, rum, tobacco and other prohibited goods and running the same on your coast.

The letter went on to provide precise details of the two vessels Robinson used in this illegal trade. One, a sloop of about 40 tons, 'painted red by the stern' and with 'a mermaid before', had just set sail from Guernsey. The other, a larger vessel of 70 to 80 tons, had three masts and was 'painted by the stern with blue and green flowers' but had 'no head afore'. This vessel, the Board advised, was 'ready to sail with the next fair wind' and had on board 1,000 lbs of tea as well as large quantities of bottled wines and kegs of brandy. The letter directed the collectors to instruct their officers to be particularly vigilant and to make every effort to prevent these vessels running in their cargoes.

Soap and candles were two other cargoes smuggled into North Devon and Somerset in considerable quantities in this period. These were commodities that carried no small Excise duty in England but could be purchased very cheaply in Ireland. Dublin was a major centre for the manufacture of both soap and candles and some of this production was illegally exported to England, severely undercutting legitimate traders. In October 1735 the Customs Board advised the Barnstaple collector that a petition had been received from the Master and Company of Chandlers and Soap Boilers at Bristol complaining that their trade was being greatly damaged by illicit imports from Ireland. These Bristol manufacturers claimed that Irish vessels were arriving at Milford Haven, Tenby and Swansea in Wales to collect coal, but were first unloading large quantities of illicit soap and candles. Some of this contraband was destined for Welsh consumers, but much was hidden on colliers bound for the Devon and Somerset coast. They also said that once landed the soap and candles were distributed inland in small parcels of one or two dozen pounds. The Customs Board directed its officials to 'be very vigilant and to use the utmost endeavour to prevent the frauds so highly detrimental to the fair trader'. Any vessel carrying coal was to be rummaged on arrival and all soap and candles found on board were to be seized. Despite this strict instruction, there are no records of Revenue officers preventing any runs of these commodities.

The elements, however, conspired to foil one attempt to smuggle soap and candles into Ilfracombe. On 24 October 1738 the Ilfracombe ship *Bedna* was caught by a gale and blown ashore on Saunton Sands. The vessel was bound for her home port, supposedly in ballast, but in fact 'a great quantity of soap and candles' was found concealed in her bulkheads and other parts of the vessel. The master of the ship, Simon Stephen, decided he would rather the 'country' had the contraband than the Customs officers so he came to an agreement with the locals to share the spoils. Eight horse-loads of soap were taken away by three armed men. Soon afterwards Customs officials found 850 pieces of soap hidden in the house of the master's sister-in-law.

War broke out with France in 1744 and this seems to have curbed smuggling in the Bristol Channel for a time. While peace negotiations were taking place in October 1748, the Barnstaple collector wrote to the Customs Board, stating:

> The smuggling trade on this coast has begun again, a vessel or two having very lately run brandy, claret &co in ... As a general peace is soon expected and very much hoped for, we are very apprehensive that this pernicious trade of smuggling will again be carried on with great impunity.

It seems likely that one of the smuggling vessels referred to was the *Molley* of Guernsey. Shortly afterwards, this ship was involved in an important smuggling incident, the story of which forms the subject of the next chapter.

3

Conflicting Evidence

In the autumn of 1748 a strange smuggling incident took place. Two different versions of the event are to be found in the pages of the Barnstaple Customs collector's book. First there is a sworn statement made by John Lake, the owner of the Ilfracombe skiff *Heart*. He described himself as an innocent party who was deceived into helping the smugglers. Then there is the affidavit of Abraham Martin, an Ilfracombe pilot. He told the story differently, giving a different location for the contraband runs and suggesting that Lake was much more involved than he admitted to. In this chapter both versions of events will be given, and the reader will be left to make a judgement as to where the truth lies.

John Lake claimed that early on the morning of Saturday 26 October a stranger approached him at the harbour. This man introduced himself as

10 Fishermen mending their nets at Porlock Weir, 1821. Fishing was a mainstay here as at several other harbours on the Exmoor coast.

John Campbell and asked if he could hire Lake to take him, his wife and some provisions out in the boatman's skiff to a brigantine lying in Lundy Roads (the sheltered waters to the east of Lundy). The sum of 12 shillings was agreed on. Lake fetched his partner George Harris and they set sail.

About midday the brigantine came into view. Lake identified this vessel in his affidavit as the *Molley* of Guernsey, although other evidence suggests she was masquerading as the *Good Hope* of Falmouth. Campbell invited the boatmen on board and paid them the 12 shillings as agreed. They talked and Campbell explained that he was the owner of the brigantine and introduced them to the master, a man named Twitty. Suddenly, Campbell offered the boatmen three guineas to carry ten ankers of brandy and rum in the skiff to the Mumbles near Swansea and to run it ashore there. Lake gives the impression that he and his partner were shocked to be asked to take part in smuggling and refused. He said Campbell then offered him and his partner 20 shillings to carry Campbell, his wife and a trunk in the skiff to Porlock. This seemed good money for lawful work so the boatmen readily agreed. They took the couple back onto the skiff, set sail and put them ashore at Porlock at five o'clock on Sunday morning.

The boatman said that three hours later he and Harris were surprised to see the *Molley* arrive in Porlock Bay. After a short while the brigantine set sail again, heading back westwards for a short distance and then dropping anchor at Coscombe Road (just offshore from Coscombe, a valley on the border between Devon and Somerset often used by smugglers and now overlooked by Glenthorne). Lake did not make it clear whether he and his partner followed in their boat. All he said in his affidavit was that the brigantine went there 'in order as he verily believed to land and run part of her cargo'.

Lake went on to say that on Monday a terrible gale blew up and the *Molley* was obliged to weigh anchor. He stated that Campbell, who was still with him on the skiff, saw that his brigantine was in grave danger and offered him to pay him handsomely if he would help save her. Lake then gave orders that the *Molley* should follow his boat. For about six hours the brigantine followed the *Heart* up the Bristol Channel. The boatman then hailed the master of the ship, and told him to steer into Woodspring Bay, south-west of Clevedon. There he showed him where to run the vessel ashore on a safe bed of mud.

Lake stated that on Tuesday, while at Woodspring, Campbell ordered the master and crew of the *Molley* to transfer 25 ankers of brandy and rum into the *Heart*. That night 19 of these ankers were taken out of the skiff and put

11 Coscombe, c.1840: a route to the interior. Smugglers sometimes carried contraband up the ravine. Glenthorne, the mansion overlooking the sea, was built for the Rev. Walter Halliday in 1830.

into the brigantine's boat. Campbell and some of the crew went off in this boat and returned to Coscombe Road. Lake and Harris apparently followed in their skiff and were in time to see Campbell helping to land the rum and brandy.

After overseeing the landing, Campbell discussed with Lake and Harris the matter of payment for all the work they had done for him. Instead of giving them the money he had promised, Campbell said they could keep four of the ankers still on the skiff for their trouble and that the other two 'should be run and disposed of by them' and the money then paid to him. The boatmen had to give Campbell a 'note-of-hand' to the value of £4 12s. to cover the money they would raise by selling his two ankers. This meant they had been drawn even further into smuggling, for they themselves would have to run in contraband and then sell it if they were to obtain the money they were owed and be able to pay Campbell the money due to him.

The two boatmen set sail back to Ilfracombe in their skiff, only to have both the skiff and ankers seized by Customs officials when they eventually reached the harbour.

Lake faced financial ruin. He finished his affidavit by telling how the following day he persuaded another boatman to take him in search of Campbell. The boatman said he found the ship owner on his vessel in Porlock Bay and told him that he and his family were now destitute. Campbell listened sympathetically to Lake and told him that if he returned to Porlock the following Tuesday, he would be given £20 for the benefit of his family. Campbell also said that if Lake would go back to Guernsey with him, and work for him there, he would be well provided for.

The sworn statement made by Albert Martin, an Ilfracombe pilot, differed in several important respects. He started by telling how Campbell, a 'Scotsman resident in Guernsey', approached him in Ilfracombe and offered to pay him two guineas to be his pilot for two weeks. Martin agreed and was taken with Campbell and his wife in Lake's skiff out to the brigantine in Lundy Roads (it is surprising that Lake in his affidavit made no mention of Martin being one of his passengers, nor indeed did he refer to him at any point in his account of events). Martin never tried to pretend he was hoodwinked into helping smugglers. Indeed, he made it clear that once on board the brigantine he saw some 45 ankers of spirits and 'tasted of the brandy several times'. He then went on to confirm that the brigantine first sailed to Porlock and from there went back as far as Coscombe Road.

At this point Martin's version of events began to differ substantially from that told by Lake. He said that at Coscombe Road ten ankers of brandy and rum were taken out of the brigantine and put into Lake's skiff, but he claimed that this 'was assigned to be run at Woodspring' rather than at Coscombe. Martin saw Campbell, Lake and Harris set sail in the skiff. He said he 'believed' the three men took it to Woodspring and landed it there.

Martin confirmed that early on Monday a storm blew up and that the brigantine then sailed from Coscombe Road and arrived at Woodspring at noon the same day. However, his version of events was then very different from Lake's, for he claimed that on Tuesday morning a local farmer called Biss went on board and made arrangements to have 25 ankers of brandy and rum smuggled ashore. He said that once it was dark a small boat belonging to Biss came alongside the brigantine. The contraband was put into the boat and rowed ashore. It was then loaded into Biss's cart, which was pulled by oxen, and 'carried into the country'.

Lake and Martin's accounts, therefore, differ significantly, particularly with respect to the location where the contraband was landed. It is difficult to ascertain where the truth lies. In Lake's favour is the fact that Harris made a sworn statement that backed his account in every important respect, though of course it could be argued that as Lake's partner he might be expected to do this. The Customs officials do not seem to have made much effort to find out which man was telling the truth. Their principal concern was to try to seize the brigantine involved in the smuggling.

The Barnstaple and Ilfracombe collectors decided to combine forces and mount a joint expedition. They hired an Ilfracombe skiff, and sent their officers off in her in search of the *Molley*. Lake went with them to act as a guide. At 5 am on 8 November the brigantine was found at Woodspring. Lake helped them bring the skiff alongside. What is surprising is that the officers then allowed him to board the vessel first. The Customs officers followed behind, but were unable to prevent the two members of crew on board making their escape ashore.

This failure to capture the smugglers is significant, for a number of other incidents will be described in this book where Customs officers seized either contraband or a smuggling vessel but did not arrest any of those involved in the smuggling. This raises the question of whether the Revenue men feared reprisals if they captured smugglers, or whether having arrested them they were bribed to release them. Another possible explanation is that the Revenue men were more interested in making seizures, for which they received prize money, than in arresting smugglers, for whom they were not well rewarded.

The two collectors certainly felt sorry for Lake, whose boat had been confiscated for smuggling. In a joint letter to the Customs Board they pleaded his case, pointing out that it was only through his assistance that they were able to find and seize the *Molley*. They suggested that Lake was deserving of pity, being 'a very poor and ignorant man with a large family, but a very honest fellow, and never before to our knowledge concerned in such an affair'. The collectors also said that all the Customs officers concerned in seizing his boat would gladly relinquish all rights of title if she could be restored to him. Finally, they pointed out that, if the Board restored his skiff to Lake, he might in return provide information 'as he and his partner are frequently out to sea and well know the places of their [the smugglers'] rendezvous'. This last remark is particularly interesting, for it makes one wonder how the two boatmen came to be so well informed about the places where smugglers met. Unfortunately, it is not possible to discover how the Board responded as the relevant letter-book has not survived.

This incident provides a fascinating insight into the mysteries and deceit involved in smuggling. It highlights the involvement of Ilfracombe boatmen and pilots, and raises the issue of where the loyalties of the local Customs officials really lay.

4

The Boom Years: 1750-1805

This chapter provides a general survey of smuggling on the Exmoor coast from 1750 to1805. This was a period when high rates of duty meant that huge profits could be made from a single successful trip. The preventive forces were still under-staffed and poorly co-ordinated, so there were fortunes to be made for those who were prepared to take a few risks.

Finding reports of contraband-running for the first part of this period proved very difficult. No Ilfracombe Customs records have survived for the years prior to 1778. There are Barnstaple letter-books for those years, but they focus on events closer to that port and stay obstinately silent on the subject of the Exmoor coast. The paucity of information should not be interpreted as indicating that there was little activity in the region. Far from it! Smuggling seems to have flourished virtually unchecked on this remote coast.

Fortunately, Graham Smith, a recent archivist at H.M. Customs and Excise, has unearthed an account of one incident in the early part of this period. He tells how in 1756 the naval sloop *Defiance* spotted an Irish wherry close in to the shore near Culbone. The naval vessel went in to investigate, knowing that vessels from Ireland were heavily involved in the supply of contraband to the Bristol Channel coast. A shot was fired across the wherry's bows to indicate that she should heave to, but the vessel failed to comply. Instead she made of with all speed down the Channel. The *Defiance* followed close on her heels, but after a long chase eventually lost her to the west of Lundy. One can imagine how disappointed the commander and crew must have been to see such a valuable prize escape them! The naval sloop then returned to Culbone and most of the sailors were put on shore to search the surrounding area for contraband. They were too late! All that was found were two broken brandy kegs and a small quantity of spoiled tea. In a report to the Customs Board on the incident, the Ilfracombe collector explained that the coastal district where the incident took place was heavily involved in smuggling, but the area was too remote to be properly policed. Here then is firm proof that contraband-running was prevalent at the time.

From 1788 the sources improve and the overriding impression is that this was a dangerous and lawless age. It was, for example, a time when armed smugglers ventured openly up the Bristol Channel to unload their cargo and then threaten local shipping. In July 1779 the Barnstaple collector informed the Customs Board that two such smuggling vessels were terrorising the local coast. One was a cutter 'carrying 18 guns of four pounds and double fortified with 32 swivels'. She was masquerading as a Boston privateer (this being the time of the American War of Independence) but the collector had 'all the reason in the world to believe it to be a smuggling vessel'. He stated that this cutter was manned by 'notorious pirates' and in the last few weeks had captured no less than six vessels, all belonging to the port of Barnstaple. Among these were the brigantine *Ann*, which had been freed on payment of a ransom of 100 guineas, and the brigantine *Sea Nymph*, which was taken a few miles east of Lundy. Local people were outraged! A petition, signed by over 60 Barnstaple merchants and masters of ships, was sent to the Customs Board demanding firm action against these armed smuggling vessels. This public pressure seems to have prompted action. In the following month the naval sloop of war *Swallow* brought into Barnstaple the sloop *Mary*, with 'twelve carriage guns of four pounds, a great number of swivels, and a chest of small arms'. It had been captured after landing a cargo of contraband just west of Padstow. Then in June 1780 the naval sloop *Lively* captured the *Swallow*, a lugger armed with eight carriage guns and laden with tea, brandy and wine, which had been found at anchor in Bude Bay.

As a war was in progress, English privateers could legally prey on enemy shipping, and Peter Fosse, the Ilfracombe collector, reported the arrival in his harbour of one foreign prize after another, often captured in distant waters and then forced up the Bristol Channel by contrary winds. Thus in October 1778 the London privateer *Revenge* arrived at Ilfracombe with two prizes. One was the *Sphinx*, a French vessel laden with sugar, coffee and ivory. The other was the *Pitt*, a London whaling ship laden with stores for the southern whaling industry, which had been captured by a French man-of-war but then recaptured by the *Revenge*. In January of the following year the Jersey privateer *Defiance* brought in the *Heureuse Marie*, a French prize in ballast. Then in November the Poole privateer *Enterprise* arrived with another French prize, the *Postillion*, laden with sugar, coffee, cocoa and cotton. In September 1780 yet another captured French vessel was brought in. This time it was *L'Amicable Catherine*, which had been taken by the Jersey privateer *Stag*.

12　Ilfracombe from Warphouse Point, c.1840. The big tidal range was a problem here as at harbours all along the Exmoor coast. Notice the two vessels under construction in the small shipbuilding yard on the left.

In such a turbulent period it is hardly surprising that the Ilfracombe pilots thought nothing of taking risks to run contraband into their harbour or into one of the remote Exmoor coves. In November 1781 Peter Fosse reported to the Customs Board:

> We think it our duty to inform you that we have received intelligence from undoubted authority, that large quantities of tea and brandy are frequently discharged out of armed smugglers from France and lodged on the island of Lundy till opportunities offer for putting the same on board pilot boats belonging to this port, and land the said goods on the coasts of Cornwall, Devon, Somerset and Wales.

Fosse suggested that the naval sloop *Beaver*, then stationed at Appledore, should be instructed to make frequent visits to Lundy and that all vessels found anchored in the bay should be searched. He particularly requested that any pilot boat from Ilfracombe found at Lundy should be thoroughly rummaged because those boats so often brought back contraband from there and ran it ashore on the local coast. The Ilfracombe collector finished by expressing concern that the armed smuggling vessels were attacking local coasting vessels after unloading their cargoes.

Time after time Peter Fosse wrote to advise London that the Ilfracombe pilot boats were heavily involved in the running of small quantities of contraband. Yet only rarely were they caught. In Chapter 6 it will be shown that three times between 1778 and 1783 the Ilfracombe pilot boat *Cornwall* was involved in smuggling. The only other Ilfracombe pilot boat seized while carrying contraband was the *Argot*, which in July 1780 was found to have a keg and several bottles of rum on board that had been obtained from an inbound merchantman from Jamaica.

These West Indiamen often carried illicit goods in addition to their authorised cargo. In November 1780 the *Alexander*, a ship bound from Jamaica to Greenock with rum and sugar on board, was forced up the Bristol Channel by 'stress of weather'. The vessel had to make an unscheduled stop at Ilfracombe harbour, where a tidesman and a boatman together seized 75 gallons of foreign rum for which there was no documentation and which some members of the crew were obviously planning to dispose of illegally.

13   Lee near Ilfracombe, c.1840. There were often reports of smuggling at this little haven. Notice the water-mill.

14   Gibraltar Cottages, Porlock Weir, 1877.

Most of the seizures made on the local coast were of relatively small quantities of contraband. In August 1780, for example, 6½ gallons of gene-va was found on the deck of the six-ton Ilfracombe vessel *Henrietta* when she arrived at Ilfracombe from St Ives. In April 1785 Edmund Fishley, an Ilfracombe tidewaiter, seized a very large cask containing 96 gallons of rum hidden in an outhouse at Watermouth Cove. The interesting point about this seizure was that the outhouse belonged to Thomas Barber Esq., a mem-ber of the local gentry. Peter Fosse wrote to the Board to say that because this gentleman was away in London he felt sure he was not party to the smuggling. One might question why he was so certain!

In June of the following year Edmund Fishley made another seizure. This time it was in an outhouse at Lee belonging to a John Beer. It consisted of a number of hampers containing 66 bottles of gin, 13 gallons of Portuguese red wine, 250 lbs. of salt and one box containing 73 packs of playing cards, curiously all missing the Ace of Spades.

Graham Smith has found that a number of Porlock vessels were caught running in small quantities of contraband on both the north and south coasts of the Bristol Channel. In 1765 the *Holly* of Porlock was seized at Ilfracombe for bringing in six tubs of spirits hidden under a cargo of fish. Then in 1772 the *Two Sisters* was caught landing packages of tobacco and jars of rum at Aberthaw on the opposite side of the Channel. Edward Michael, the master, attempted to bribe the Customs officer to overlook the incident with the offer of a jar of rum. Likewise at Newport in 1790 the Porlock smack *Adventure* was seized for landing six ankers of brandy and ten packages of tobacco at the entrance to the River Ebbw. John Thetone, the owner and master, had hidden the contraband in a specially constructed compartment in the bulkhead.

It is worth mentioning here that a Porlock surgeon seems to have had a financial interest in a smuggling vessel. In 1787 the sloop *Nancy* was built at Mevagissey in Cornwall. The vessel was registered at Minehead in March 1789 but then in January 1790 she was re-registered at Fowey in Cornwall. The principal shareholders were two gentlemen from St Austell, the master, also from St Austell, a mariner from Plymouth Dock and Henry Philps, the Porlock surgeon. In the following year this vessel was seized for smuggling and condemned. One wonders how many other prominent Exmoor people had a financial stake in smuggling ventures.

In 1786 an attempt to run in a large consignment of contraband at Heddon's Mouth was foiled. An Irish wherry was in the process of discharging a cargo of spirits and tobacco onto the beach when a party of Customs officers surprised the smugglers. A struggle broke out but the officers eventually managed to seize 20 ankers of spirits and 13 bales of tobacco. The wherry made good her escape. She was believed to belong to Thomas Knight, a notorious Welsh smuggler who was reported to be using Lundy as his base.

About this time the Excise cutter *Ferret* was stationed at Milford Haven and began patrolling the Bristol Channel together with the western approaches. The Ilfracombe collector's books record the cutter bringing into his harbour a number of seized smuggling vessels with very substantial cargoes of contraband, but unfortunately the details are skimpy and never record the location where they were captured. However, it is reasonable to assume that she would only have brought into Ilfracombe those smuggling vessels taken within easy reach of the port.

Ilfracombe harbour had never seen such a flurry of seizures! The *Ferret* began in November 1788 by bringing in the sloop *Four Brothers* of Mevagissey with an illicit cargo of brandy and geneva. In January of the following year she escorted in the *Success* of Padstow. The latter had on board 1,085 lbs. of manufactured tobacco and 280 lbs. of snuff. An unusual feature of this seizure was that the contraband was neatly packed in bladders, suggesting that it was to have been sunk at some point along the coast for future collection by a local boat. In February the cutter brought in the *Polly* of Cardiff with 505 lbs. of manufactured tobacco and 12,295 lbs of unprocessed tobacco on board. Two months later the *Ferret* captured the skiff *Morning Star* of Bristol, which was carrying 1,557 lbs of unprocessed tobacco. Another vessel taken in by the Excise cutter about this time was the *Three Friends* of St Ives, with a cargo of brandy, rum and geneva on board.

When it is considered that the *Ferret* would also have taken captured vessels and contraband into her home port of Milford Haven, and may also have taken seizures to the Customs ports of St Ives, Padstow and Bideford, the scale of the smuggling at this time becomes apparent. It is clear that large quantities of contraband were being brought into the Bristol Channel and one can fairly assume that some of these cargoes were destined for places along the Exmoor coast. The fact that smugglers were only rarely caught landing them simply reflects the lack of any riding officers to police the region.

After a seizure was made it was left to the Court of the Exchequer in London to determine whether a particular vessel and her cargo should be condemned, that is confiscated, or if there were extenuating circumstances to warrant a more lenient course of action. The Ilfracombe collector's books provide sufficient information to reveal the fate of some of the vessels and cargoes the *Ferret* captured. They show that the *Four Brothers* and the *Three Friends* were both condemned and then put up for sale in Ilfracombe. The Board ordered that all the tobacco seized from the *Success*, *Polly* and *Morning Star* was to be burnt.

Further seizures made by Excise cutters were brought into Ilfracombe in the 1790s, but the Customs collector doesn't mention them in his letters, probably because the Excise took responsibility for disposing of both condemned contraband and vessels. The evidence for these seizures is found in advertisements for sales at the Britannia Inn, Ilfracombe, placed by the Excise in the pages of the *Exeter Flying Post*. In April 1796, for example, the Excise advertised the sale of 200 gallons of brandy, 3 gallons of rum, 15 gallons of geneva and 112 lbs of soap. In the following month a sale was advertised for the broken-up hulls of the *Prosperous*, a cutter, and the *Lively*, a skiff, both vessels having been seized and condemned.

Another fragment of evidence for smuggling continuing in this period comes from the pen of William Hazlitt. He describes an encounter in 1798 with a 'scowling' smuggler while accompanying Samuel Taylor Coleridge on a long walk along the Exmoor coast to visit Lynton and Lynmouth.

By 1800 smuggling had reached epidemic proportions. In March the Barnstaple collector complained that more than 50 horses were being used to transport contraband landed on the local coasts at night. Four months later the naval cutter *Dover* captured the Bideford sloop *Endeavour* and took her into Ilfracombe harbour. On board were 1,076 gallons of brandy, 500 gallons of geneva, 225 gallons of rum and five hundredweight of white salt. The vessel, her tackle and contraband were condemned. One can imagine what a financial blow that must have been to the owner. Daniel Johnson, the master, escaped to Guernsey, but whether this was to avoid the angry owner or to escape prosecution is not clear. The Ilfracombe collector advised London that the sloop was not well suited for smuggling but would make a good fishing boat. He recommended that the boat be 'sold entire' as this would 'be advantageous to the Crown, the seizing officer and his crew'. The Board took his advice and the *Endeavour* was sold at public auction to a fisherman.

Two significant seizures were made on land in the months that followed. In October 1800 Edmund Fishley, coastwaiter, and Thomas Scamp, tidesman, discovered 12 bags containing 1,320 lbs. of unprocessed tobacco at Warcombe in the parish of Ilfracombe. This tobacco was condemned and sold at public auction in December. Then in April 1801 Customs officers discovered 32 small casks holding 224 gallons of gin and 23 small casks containing 164 gallons of brandy on the seashore in the parish of Ilfracombe. No further details are given in the records but it would seem that a landing had been interrupted.

Tragedy struck later that month. The sloop *Hope* had successfully landed 96 ankers of spirits at Heddon's Mouth and was in the process of moving from there to Watermouth Cove to discharge the remainder of her cargo. The vessel probably struck a submerged rock as she kept close inshore to avoid being seen from the top of the cliffs. She went down with all hands. An event such as this highlights the hazardous nature of smuggling. All eight members of the crew lost their lives. The Ilfracombe collector reported that all except Daniel Johnson, the master, were from the Ilfracombe area. Could this Daniel Johnson be the same ship's master who in the previous year had fled to Guernsey when his vessel *Endeavour* was seized for smuggling?

Other seizures followed. In September 1801 James Wood, commander of the Revenue cutter *Racer*, then moored in Ilfracombe harbour, became suspicious that the sloop *Four Brothers* had contraband on board. He sent

15   The 'safe haven' of Watermouth Cove in 1832. In 1801 the smuggling vessel *Hope* went down with all hands while approaching the cove with a cargo of spirits.

some of his crew to search the vessel and they found two ankers of illicit spirits. One wonders if the commander took action because he felt the port officials were not doing their job properly. Then in August 1804 the Revenue cutter *Shark* surprised the Bideford brigantine *Margaretta* at Woody Bay in the act of unloading a large cargo of illicit goods from Guernsey (an incident described in Chapter 8).

In December 1804 John Litt, the Barnstaple collector, wrote a long letter to the Customs Board in which he stressed the magnitude of the problem and pointed out that smuggling was increasing rather than decreasing during the war with France. He also made it clear that most of the smuggling vessels were obtaining their contraband from Guernsey and spelled out the problems that Revenue cutters like the *Shark* were up against:

We find that smuggling in general has for some years been increasing and is carried on at present on the coasts of Devon and Cornwall to an alarming extent. These spirits are imported from Guernsey, chiefly in cutters and luggers, professedly on the smuggling trade, which are so well constructed and manned as to outsail most of the Revenue cruisers. The cargoes of these vessels consist generally of from 400 to 800 ankers of spirits, a few casks of port and sherry wine and some small bales of tobacco.

An interesting feature of this letter is that by this time the smuggling vessels were no longer described as being armed. The smugglers had realised they could no longer hope to outgun the Revenue cutters and instead had begun to rely solely on speed and superior seamanship to enable them to escape when chased.

The collector went on to explain that in winter it was very dangerous to try to land contraband on the exposed Cornish coast and it was at that time of the year that smuggling vessels were more likely to run in their cargoes on the Exmoor coast. He listed the main landing places and explained that the contraband was then transported across the moor:

As these vessels are prevented from landing in the winter season on the Cornish coast, which is very dangerous and then rendered inaccessible with safety, through the prevalence of strong westerly winds, they run further up the Bristol Channel ...The principal places of landing on this side of the Channel are Clovelly (a place notorious for its smuggling), Combe Martin, Lee, Lynmouth, Withy [Woody] Bay and Porlock, extending upwards of twenty miles, on no part of which, we understand, is a single officer of the Customs stationed, and having a near connection with Exmoor. The goods are conveyed across that Forest into the county of Somerset.

He pointed out that in addition to the many fast, purpose-built smuggling vessels active along local coasts, some 'common coasting vessels' such as the *Margaretta* had begun sailing to Guernsey to obtain an illegal cargo and after taking on board contraband they had their hatchways covered with limestone or coal to avoid suspicion. Then he went on to recommend the appointment of a riding officer to patrol the Exmoor coast from Morte Point to Minehead. Finally, he claimed that the smugglers were helped by having the support of most of the local inhabitants and by the fact that most of the local customs officers were not doing their job properly.

Several smuggling incidents occurred in the early months of 1805, reinforcing the Barnstaple collector's warning that contraband running was widespread in the region. First, in January, shortly after taking up station at Ilfracombe, the Excise cutter *Resolution* seized 260 lbs. of pepper, but the

16 Advertisement in the *Exeter Flying Post* for seized contraband offered for public sale at Ilfracombe by the Excise. The Excise cutter *Resolution*, which at the time was stationed at Ilfracombe, would almost certainly have been responsible for the seizure of the goods.

Customs books provide no details of the place or circumstances. Then on 10 March the *Shark* and her boats left Ilfracombe harbour and after a remarkable chase seized the *Dart*, carrying a cargo of spirits, tobacco and pepper from Guernsey (an incident described in Chapter 8). Later in the year this Customs cutter would also capture other smuggling vessels on the Cornish coast.

On the same day that the *Shark* captured the lugger *Dart*, the Excise cutter *Resolution* chased but lost another large smuggling lugger. After this vessel escaped, she took her cargo of over 600 ankers of spirits to Lynmouth. The Barnstaple collector reported to the Customs Board that she ran in close to the quay, 'where she grounded and in the face of day landed her whole cargo, which remained in an open field for two days afterwards, unknown to any Revenue officer, before it was conveyed away by the smugglers'. There could at the time have been few places in England where the smugglers could leave contraband out in the open so blatantly and for so long without fear of detection! In his letter to the Board the Barnstaple collector pointed out that the coast between Ilfracombe and Minehead was 'a great resort of smugglers' and once again strongly recommended the appointment of a rid-ing officer to patrol the coast. He finished by saying that since the incident he had 'personally surveyed' the whole of the Exmoor coast and, though he found it to be in some places 'mountainous', he was 'satisfied of the practi-cality of its being safely travelled' should the Board see fit to appoint a

17 The harbour at Lynmouth in 1813. A large cargo of over 600 ankers of spirits was brought into this isolated fishing village in 1805, and left in a field for two days without any Revenue officers being aware of the landing.

riding officer. His suggestion was not taken up and the region remained unguarded.

Yet another incident of 1805 requires a mention. In July Samuel Bremeridge, a Barnstaple landing waiter, seized four bags of Spanish wool, which were in the process of being loaded on the stage wagon at Barnstaple to be sent to Chard. The Barnstaple collector later explained that the wool had been seized on suspicion of its having been 'clandestinely landed' from a vessel lying at Ilfracombe. This seizure followed a number of reports that large quantities of Spanish wool had been moved from Ilfracombe to inland districts, despite the fact that no wool had been legally landed there.

The years between 1800 and 1805 seem to have marked the zenith of smuggling on the Exmoor coast. These were certainly the years when recorded incidents reached a peak. Thereafter smuggling seems to have entered a long period of decline. Never again would contraband be run in so openly and easily. In the years that followed, the preventive forces would gradually gain the upper hand in their long battle with the smugglers.

5

The Lundy Connection

Lundy: so small and yet so important as a source of Exmoor contraband. Bulk consignments of spirits and wine arrived at the desolate island on large sailing ships from France and the Channel Islands. Small cargoes were then picked up by Ilfracombe pilot boats or local coasting vessels, which could land them in Exmoor harbours and creeks without attracting attention. The island also had an important trade in illicit tobacco.

At first sight Lundy might seem quite unsuitable for use as a smuggler's base. Granite cliffs rise steeply from the Atlantic while the interior is bleak and rocky. In fact the island's inhospitable nature was one of its principal attractions for the contraband runner, as this meant it was virtually uninhabited. Furthermore, on the south-eastern tip of the island lay a sheltered cove providing protection from westerly gales. Lundy also had an excellent strategic position, commanding the western approaches to the Bristol Channel and being ideally placed to supply not just North Devon and Somerset but also South Wales.

Lundy first began to be used by smugglers after Richard Score leased it in 1721. Yet only once during his period of occupancy did the Customs succeed in making a seizure. The Customs records show that in December 1727 a William Cuthbert was prosecuted for being caught there with two hogsheads and 50 gallons of wine. A judgement was obtained against him, but by his name on a document was written 'he could not be taken'. Smuggling seems to have come to a temporary stop when Score left the island at the end of the decade and for many years it was uninhabited.

It was Thomas Benson who turned Lundy into a fortified smugglers' base. In 1743 this merchant had inherited Knapp House, on the hill above Appledore, together with an estate and, most importantly, a fleet of over a dozen ships operating out of Barnstaple and Bideford. Benson traded principally with the North American colonies, but also with the Mediterranean. His vessels brought back tobacco from Virginia and Maryland, cod from Newfoundland and wine from Portugal. So successful was his trade with the American colonies that for a time more tobacco was being imported into Bideford than into any other port in England except London. Benson became a powerful man. In 1746 he was made Sheriff of

18 The desolate island of Lundy, 1895. Gloomy cliffs seemed to warn off approaching vessels. Marisco Castle commanded one of the few paths up from the sea.

the county of Devon and in the following year he was elected Member of Parliament for Barnstaple. He then used his influence in government circles to obtain a lucrative contract to transport convicts to Virginia and Maryland at £20 per head, which meant that his vessels had a guaranteed cargo in both directions.

Underneath his façade of wealth, power and political influence, Benson was a rogue. He hatched a scheme to avoid paying import duties on much of his tobacco. His ships would arrive home from Virginia and Maryland with a cargo of tobacco. This was stored in a bonded warehouse at Barnstaple or Bideford, but then Benson would have it released without paying Customs duty by swearing an oath that it was to be exported. Time after time his ships left Barnstaple and Bideford ostensibly bound for a European destination, only for the tobacco to be run ashore at some point on the Bristol Channel coast.

In 1748 Benson hit on the idea of leasing Lundy from its owner, Lord Gower. This meant that when his ships left Barnstaple and Bideford with duty-free tobacco they could deposit it on the island to await collection by a local boat. Not content with this, Benson thought of a scheme that would provide him with slave labour. Some of the convicts he was being paid to take to the American colonies found themselves being taken no further than Lundy. There they were set to work fortifying the island and adapting caves for use as storehouses for his contraband tobacco. Then they were employed in opening the hogsheads of tobacco that his ships illegally landed, removing the waste and then dividing the tobacco into smaller parcels more convenient for smuggling in on the coasts of North Devon, Somerset and South Wales.

Yet despite all his scheming, things did not go well for Benson. By 1748 it seems that the heavy costs he had incurred in buying power and political position had left him short of money, for in that year the Customs' correspondence had a growing number of references to Benson's unpaid tobacco bonds. Previously, the Barnstaple Customs officers had allowed their borough's leading merchant to carry on his illegal trade unchecked, but now they felt obliged to keep a close watch on his activities. In 1749 they demanded £992 in duty and penalties from Benson for tobacco illegally imported in his ship *Grace*. In the years that followed he was caught out time after time trying to defraud the Customs until he owed the king the staggering sum of £8,229. He was desperate to find ways of raising money.

In October 1751 Benson had a large cargo of 60 hogsheads of tobacco taken out of the bonded warehouse in Barnstaple without paying duty, on the pretext that it was going to be exported to Morlaix in Brittany. His brigantine *Vine*, with John Clibbert master, left Barnstaple with the tobacco, put in at Milford Haven and then set sail, supposedly for France, but only six days later arrived empty at Burry Port, near Llanelli. In so short a time it was virtually impossible for the vessel to have sailed to Brittany, discharged its cargo and then sailed back. The Customs officials strongly suspected that the tobacco had been taken to Lundy.

Four Barnstaple Customs officials went out to Lundy, but arrived too late. It seems Benson had been tipped off and both tobacco and convicts had been removed from the island. Yet the officers saw enough to convince them that a considerable quantity of tobacco had recently been landed there in hogsheads and unpacked, as there were a number of staves lying about and waste tobacco was scattered on the ground. These suspicions were confirmed when, shortly afterwards, 1,132 lbs. of tobacco were seized at Appledore in Benson's ship *Dolphin*. A few days later at Ilfracombe a large fishing vessel was seized for being laden with illicit tobacco, almost certainly from the same source. In the same period smaller quantities of tobacco were found hidden in houses, barns and thickets just inland from the North Devon coast. One wonders how many cargoes Benson had smuggled in before the authorities began to check up on him.

Shortly afterwards, Benson's ship *Catherine* arrived at Instow with a cargo of tobacco from Maryland, and the Barnstaple Customs officials carefully checked the contents. They found that most of the hogsheads had been opened and that the weight of tobacco inside them was much less than listed on the manifest. The master claimed that while still in Maryland the vessel had sprung a leak and that the tobacco had had to be emptied out and dried. He made the lame excuse that some of the tobacco must have been stolen while this was being done. However, the Customs officials suspected that the missing tobacco had been unlawfully landed elsewhere, probably at Lundy.

In the following year the Customs Commissioners received more information about Benson's activities on Lundy and this time there was even a warning that the island was being fortified:

The Commissioners have received information from a gentleman in South Wales that a new trade is carried on at the island of Lundy and that many ships outward bound from Barnstaple Bay unload there and that the cargoes are afterwards returned to that country in other vessels, that a platform with guns is being erected and shot fired to bring ships to, for to account who and what they are … unless an immediate stop be put to it, the island will become a magazine for smugglers.

In July of that year, several wealthy friends of Benson were invited to visit Lundy. An anonymous member of the group wrote a remarkable account of their stay. He described seeing convicts building a wall on the island and then being locked up at night in a fort. He said that, a week prior to their visit, seven or eight of the convicts had escaped in a rowing boat to Hartland on the mainland. The visitor described a cave where Benson 'lodged his goods'. On one occasion the party saw almost 20 ships enter Lundy Roads. Benson had his colours hoisted on the fort and all the vessels returned the compliment except one. He was so angry with the offending ship that he fired cannon balls at it!

Even while this party was on the island, Benson was making the final arrangements for a desperate scheme to pay off his massive debts to the Customs. He had decided to heavily insure the *Nightingale*, one of the oldest ships in his fleet, together with her cargo, secretly unload the brigantine at Lundy, have her set on fire and sunk, and then claim the insurance money. The anonymous visitor wrote in his account that Benson had not at first accompanied his guests to the island because he was 'expecting letters from his insurance office' for his ship, which was lying at 'his quay with convicts bound for Virginia'.

On 28 July 1752, only a few days after the visitors had left the island, the *Nightingale* set sail from Barnstaple with John Lancey, one of his most trusted captains, on board as master. Benson watched her go down the estuary from the grounds of Knapp House. The brigantine duly arrived at Lundy, exchanged signals with the fort and came to anchor in the bay. All Benson's cargo of broadcloth, linen, nails and assorted domestic goods was put ashore with only 350 bushels of salt shipped for a customer being left on board. The ship then weighed anchor and sailed.

Some 50 miles west of Lundy, Lancey ordered holes to be bored in his ship's hull and had her set on fire. The convicts were put in the longboat and then the crew joined them. They were picked up by a passing ship and eventually put ashore at Clovelly. Benson was delighted when Captain Lancey arrived back at Knapp House and reported that all had gone well. Unfortunately for him, the boatswain turned informer. Lancey and some of his crew were then arrested.

Thomas Benson was now in desperate trouble. Fearing the sailors would confirm the boatswain's story, he tried to buy their silence by telling them he would have them released on bail and then help them escape the country. Yet in reality he was not in a position to raise the bail money, for his financial problems were mounting. In February 1753 judgement was given against him at the Court of Exchequer for the £8,229 claimed by the Customs. When the news broke, creditors besieged his London house.

The worried merchant also feared there were moves afoot to prosecute him for using Lundy for smuggling. It was probably to try to prevent this that in March he petitioned the Commissioners of the Treasury to have the island recognised as a legal landing place for goods. The Commissioners of the Customs were asked for their view and in May responded with a report making it clear that they were only too aware the island was being used for the running of contraband:

The smuggling trade has been revived there, and goods have been frequently landed on the island ...The island of Lundy by its situation is very convenient for smuggling, as it lies in the midway between England

and Wales, so that from there goods may be run on either side of the Channel with all the ease imaginable, and especially if a pier was to be built as proposed by the memorialist, for the shelter of small vessels, which are usually employed on such occasions … We are of the opinion the Revenue will be exposed to very great frauds should the island of Lundy be established a lawful place for the ordinary shipping and landing of goods.

Benson's problems mounted. His Lundy application was dismissed. Then his estates were seized as security for his debts to the Crown. He now feared that Captain Lancey and the other prisoners would realise he was unable to help them and decide to turn king's evidence against him. Early in December he took flight to Portugal, leaving Lancey and his fellow prisoners to their fate.

In July 1754 John Lancey was hanged at Execution Dock after having been found guilty of having unlawfully destroyed the *Nightingale*. The captain had been made the scapegoat, for his only crime had been to loyally carry out his employer's orders. The two other men put on trial escaped the gallows, but must have felt bitter that their employer had deserted them in their time of need.

Benson meanwhile was busy creating a new life in Oporto. There is no way of telling whether he was troubled by guilt. What is known is that he arranged for two of his ships to join him there and that he used them to establish a new merchant business. Hitherto, it has generally been believed he never dared set foot in England again. However, in conducting research for this book, evidence has come to light suggesting Benson may have returned to England for a time and actually stayed at Knapp House. In February 1765 the Barnstaple collector wrote to the Customs Board as follows:

We think it our duty to acquaint your honours that it is strongly suspected, and we believe not without foundation, that Mr Thomas Benson (who stands indebted to the Crown in several thousand pounds on account of tobacco bonds) is actually at his house at Northam.

The reply from the Customs House was surprising. Despite the fact that Benson was known to have been a smuggler on a massive scale, and the perpetrator of the *Nightingale* fraud, the collector was instructed not to try to arrest him because 'no benefit would accrue to the Crown if Benson was taken'. Did he still have influential friends in high places?

Thomas Benson died in exile in Oporto at the age of 64. He will always be remembered for his shameful part in the *Nightingale* scandal. But he was also the man who turned Lundy into a fortified smugglers' base and perpetrated the biggest Customs frauds North Devon has ever known.

Benson had gone, but Lundy remained a dangerous, lawless place. In 1775 Sir John Warren bought the island for only £510 and immediately began strengthening its defences. The records show that in July of the following year he landed cannon, mortars, shot, shells, muskets, pistols, blunderbusses, cutlasses, bayonets and gunpowder on the island. What they fail to make clear is whether Warren needed all this armour to protect smugglers or to keep him safe from them when they landed.

Certainly the evidence shows Lundy was still being used as a smuggling base. In 1776, for example, the Barnstaple collector received information that two smuggling vessels had called there and that they had on board illicit cargoes 'intended to be run in the Bristol Channel'. In November 1782 the Swansea collector advised London that a search of the island had revealed 128 ankers of brandy and four bags of Bohea tea (black China tea of the finest quality) hidden in caves and huts. He said there was a very considerable smuggling trade on the island. Three times in 1783 the Ilfracombe collector reported that armed cutters were taking contraband to Lundy and that pilot boats were then bringing this to Ilfracombe or running it ashore at other places on the local coast. In 1785 the Cardiff collector informed the Customs Board that Thomas Knight, a notorious Welsh smuggler, was believed to have made Lundy his base after finally being driven from his stronghold on Barry Island.

Not until the very end of the century did the smugglers finally abandon Lundy. An increase in the number of Revenue cutters patrolling the Bristol Channel meant that smuggling vessels could no longer sail unchallenged to the island and lie offshore while they discharged their contraband. With Lundy under constant surveillance by Customs officers, the smugglers found it safer not to call there and instead took their cargoes directly to remote bays on the mainland. The days when the Exmoor coast obtained its contraband from Lundy had at last come to an end.

6

The Pilot Vessel *Cornwall*

The Ilfracombe pilot vessels were heavily involved in the running of contraband at the time Lundy was flourishing as a smugglers' base. Yet
accounts of smuggling by these pilot vessels are hard to find, as only rarely
were they caught in the act. The *Cornwall*, an Ilfracombe pilot boat of some
20 tons, has been chosen as the subject of this chapter because three times
the Ilfracombe collector, Peter Fosse, managed to find evidence to prove
that she had been involved in the running in of contraband.

Before embarking on the story it seems appropriate to provide a little
background material about the pilot boats and their methods of operation.
They had unique opportunities for smuggling. It was their task to meet the
ships entering the Bristol Channel and then put a pilot aboard to help nav-
igate. So they had a legitimate reason to rendezvous with West Indiamen
laden with rum and sugar, and likewise with ships inward bound from
Maryland and Virginia with tobacco, or from Europe carrying brandy and
gin. Furthermore, it was known that the masters and officers of some of
these incoming ships supplemented their income by trading on their own
account. The pilot boats also had a valid reason for heading out towards
Lundy, for it was in those waters that they often met incoming ships. This
gave them the perfect opportunity to pick up illicit goods on the island.

There were a number of reasons why the pilot boats were rarely caught
smuggling. First, they sailed far to the west to meet an incoming ship so as
to be outside the six-mile territorial limit when they picked up contraband.
This meant the Revenue cutters were powerless to intervene if they
suspected an illegal transaction was taking place. Secondly, once the pilot
boats had contraband on board they were unlikely to be caught while out
at sea, for they were fast and could usually out-sail any Revenue cutter.
Thirdly, the pilots had an unrivalled knowledge of the local coasts, bays and
tidal currents. It is significant that the only reported seizures from pilot
boats came when they risked running contraband into Ilfracombe itself,
instead of into some remote bay.

John Lovering was master of the *Cornwall* on the first occasion that she
was found in Ilfracombe harbour with contraband on board. One day in
August 1778 he had set out from Ilfracombe in his skiff to meet a ship from

19   Pilots at Ilfracombe harbour in 1859. They were probably going to row out to a pilot cutter.

Jamaica bound for Bristol. His official reason for going out had been to put a pilot aboard the West Indiaman, but having done this he had collected 13 gallons of rum, 6 lbs. of tea and 84 lbs. of sugar and brought them back to Ilfracombe. Lovering took the calculated risk of leaving the contraband on deck as he berthed, but, unluckily for him, it was spotted by a vigilant Customs official.

In his defence, Lovering claimed he had obtained the goods 'from several persons on board' the West Indiaman and that he had been requested to bring it to land 'as presents to their friends and acquaintances' in Ilfracombe. It seems, however, much more likely that he had purchased the goods from the crew of the ship and was smuggling them in. This was certainly the view the Customs officers took. They confiscated the goods but, because no attempt had been made to conceal them, the boat itself was not liable to be forfeited.

Another seizure involving the *Cornwall* took place in 1782. In November of that year Peter Fosse sent the Customs Board an inventory of a quantity of brandy and tea that some of his officers had seized near the harbour in Ilfracombe. In an accompanying letter he said he had 'great reason to think that the goods therein mentioned were landed out of a pilot boat belonging to this port'. While patrolling the harbour, some Customs officers had seen William Thorne, a rope-maker, carrying one of the casks towards an outhouse belonging to John Marshall. He appeared to be coming from the *Cornwall*, which was anchored nearby. The officers were not able to discover who else had been involved, but had found both tea and brandy casks hidden in Marshall's outhouse. After further searches they discovered more brandy and tea stored in another outhouse, this time belonging to Samuel Cornish. This name is significant, for a Samuel Cornish was the master of the *Cornwall* when she was caught with contraband on board in the following year. It seems that the Customs officers took no action against either of the two outhouse owners because it could not be proved they were aware the contraband was stored there.

The third incident involving the *Cornwall* occurred in April 1783. Edmund Fishley, a tidesman, accompanied by two Customs boatmen, went on board the skiff in Ilfracombe harbour and found three half-ankers of geneva. They brought the contraband ashore and stored it 'in the King's warehouse under lock'. The Customs officers then went back to the pilot boat and searched it more thoroughly. This time they found a small case of geneva, which the crew claimed was for their own use. When this was reported to the Customs collector, he suspected that there might be still more contraband hidden on board, so he ordered other officers to go back and 'rummage' again. This time they found four canvas bags containing 48 lbs. of Bohea tea concealed in the foresheets of the pilot boat. This tea they seized together with the small case of geneva. More importantly the officers also took possession of the *Cornwall*, as they were entitled to do because the contraband had been concealed on board.

The Customs Board soon afterwards received a petition from a Mr William Arthur of Pennard in the Gower, South Wales. He said he was the owner of the *Cornwall* and asked that the vessel 'be delivered up' to him, because he said the tea and geneva had been put on board without either his knowledge or consent or that of Samuel Cornish, the master. He also enclosed affidavits from John Groves and John Andrew, two of the crew of the pilot boat. These stated that the tea had been purchased at sea by them and other members of the crew without the knowledge of the master, and that both the tea and geneva had been 'put on board without the privity and consent' of either Arthur or Cornish.

Peter Fosse wrote back to the Board disputing the points made in Arthur's petition. He said that before the *Cornwall* had been purchased by Arthur she had been employed in piloting and fishing, but since then she had been 'employed by him in an illicit trade between the island of Lundy and the coasts of Cornwall, Devon, Somerset and Wales in the Bristol Channel'. He stated there was 'great reason to think that the seizure of tea and brandy made by the officers here in the month of November last came out of the said boat, as she lay at anchor near the place where the seizure was made'. He also pointed out that affidavits sworn by two of the crew members could not be correct because Samuel Cornish, the master, must have been present while the contraband was being purchased at sea and transferred to the skiff. Furthermore, Cornish must have seen the tea when it was hidden under the foresheets as this was where he and his crew slept and ate together.

The Customs Board rejected William Arthur's application for the release of his skiff. A decision then had to be taken as to what should be done with the vessel. In cases like this the officers concerned in the seizure were very keen that she should be sold, as in that case they received a proportion of the money obtained. However, the Board had a policy of breaking up any vessel that might subsequently be used again for smuggling and in such cases the officers received a smaller reward. The *Cornwall* was obviously ideally suited to be used in the smuggling trade so, sadly for the officers concerned, she was condemned, sawn in three and the materials sold off to defray expenses.

The decision not to return the skiff to Arthur was the correct one. Years later it was discovered he was the leader of a large gang involved in many of the Bristol Channel's biggest smuggling operations. Arthur was based in South Wales and by August 1788 the Swansea Customs collector was describing him as a 'notorious smuggler'. Many Customs officers went in fear of him. His farms on the Gower coast were finally raided in April 1804 and concealed cellars packed with contraband were found. After the raid the Swansea collector said it was believed that from these properties the Bristol Channel region had been 'supplied many years with foreign spirits and other uncustomed goods to a vast amount'. He also reported: 'Arthur it is generally understood has realised a large fortune by that trade and has purchased an estate in Devonshire to which he occasionally retires.'

This reference to William Arthur having a Devon estate is interesting, for he disappears from Welsh smuggling records after this major raid and it is possible that he spent his last years living the life of a gentleman on the south side of the Bristol Channel. This brings to mind a reference by the Ilfracombe collector in 1814 to a wealthy local resident 'believed to have been formerly engaged in the illegal running of goods'. The collector wrote of this mysterious figure: 'He lives in a state of independence, has no family, is advanced in years and has a good property.' Might this just possibly have been be William Arthur, the one-time leader of a Welsh smuggling gang and former owner of an Ilfracombe pilot boat?

The seizure of the *Cornwall* did little to discourage the other Ilfracombe pilots from smuggling. In October 1783 Peter Fosse sent a letter to the Board in which he actually named some of the worst culprits and pleaded that more Revenue vessels might be sent to cruise along the local coast. He wrote:

> We are well assured that most of the pilot boats belonging to this port are concerned in these illicit practices, but John Hodge, master of the *Lundy Pilot*, Samuel Cornish Junior, master of the *Hero*, and Peter Allen, master of the *Bristol Galley*, (three of the said boats) are entirely engaged in running goods on the coasts in the Bristol Channel, which cannot be prevented by the Officers here, or a greater number if established, but by the vigilance of the cruisers that may be appointed by Government for that purpose.

Despite the fact that the collector knew only too well which pilot boats were principally involved in the running in of contraband, there were no further seizures after this date. The smugglers still had the upper hand, and the Customs officials seemed either unable or unwilling to prevent their illegal activities.

7

The War on Smuggling: 1805-1835

The Government launched an all-out war on smuggling in the period beginning 1805. There had been growing concern at the mushrooming problem of contraband running and this led to a whole series of new measures aimed at curbing it. The result was a sudden drop in smuggling activity on the Exmoor coast. The tide of battle changed in favour of the preventive officers and the smugglers were forced to become even more furtive when running in a cargo.

The first and most important step taken was to cut off the main source of supply. Guernsey had long been an important source of contraband because it was exempt from Customs and Excise levies. In other words it was a duty-free island, conveniently placed to obtain goods from France. The majority of the bulk cargoes of contraband entering the Bristol Channel originated from there. In times of war, when it was dangerous or impossible for English vessels to visit French ports, the island had taken on even more importance as a supplier of contraband. In 1805, however, the British Parliament decreed that Guernsey, along with the other Channel Islands, was at last to be subject to Customs law and duties. What a blow for the smugglers that was! The fact that Britain was at war made matters worse, for this meant there were considerable risks involved in trying to obtain alternative supplies direct from France. Yet the imposition of Customs control on Guernsey did not completely eliminate smuggling. Napoleon began to actively encourage English contraband runners to buy supplies at French ports, because his country desperately needed the gold their trade provided.

Another factor that contributed to the decrease in smuggling on the Exmoor coast was the success enjoyed by Captain Matthews and his crew on the Revenue cutter *Shark* (a detailed account is provided in Chapter 8). Between 1804 and 1807 this cutter seized one smuggling ship after another. The news spread along the south-west coast and contraband runners must have questioned whether they wanted to risk meeting the *Shark* on the long journey to North Devon and Somerset.

Parliament dealt the smugglers another blow when in 1806 it passed legislation rendering all luggers exceeding 50 tons and built in the United Kingdom illegal and forfeit. This was a real blow for the contraband runners, for these fast-sailing, robust and capacious ships had been ideally suited for carrying large quantities of illicit freight on long voyages. In fact the majority of the vessels bringing contraband to the Exmoor coast had been of this type.

These preventive measures had an immediate impact. In 1807 the Barnstaple collector reported to the Customs Board that there had been not a single recent case of smuggling on his section of the coast, whereas only three years earlier he had been warning that smuggling was being carried on to 'an alarming extent'. He did point out, however, that 'considerable quantities of spirits' were still being 'frequently landed further up the Bristol Channel within the ports of Ilfracombe and Minehead, the whole sea coast of which is perfectly unguarded'.

Further evidence that some smuggling was still taking place on the Exmoor coast came in a letter from the Customs Board to local collectors in February 1808. It advised them that the Minehead sloop *Venture* was making its way to Ireland to load salt, which it would then try to smuggle in. Customs officers were instructed to keep a good look out for the vessel 'to prevent any fraud being committed'.

Two further preventive measures helped to reduce smuggling on Exmoor. In 1810 the national Preventive Waterguard was established. One of their rowing galleys was stationed at Porlock and from there was well placed to police local inshore waters. Two years later a riding officer was finally appointed to ride along a large section of the Exmoor coast. His name was Benjamin Stevens and he was based at Lynmouth. His brief was to patrol the long stretch of coast from the county boundary in the east to Combe Martin in the west. With him on the lookout on land and members of the Waterguard keeping watch just off the coast, it was obviously going to be much more difficult for smugglers to run in their cargoes.

By this time smuggling on the Exmoor coast was certainly on the decline. Between 1810 and 1815 there were only two recorded seizures, both at Ilfracombe. In August 1813 two casks of wine were found floating in the sea near the port. Then in the following year a quantity of French lace and silk handkerchiefs was seized from a Guernsey ship moored by the pier after she had been forced in by 'contrary winds'. The commander of an excise cutter stationed in the port had found the goods while rummaging through the vessel's cargo after receiving a tip-off that there was contraband on board.

When Napoleon was finally defeated at Waterloo in June 1815, there were real fears that the contraband trade would revive, because, with the return of peace, English smugglers could safely visit French ports and

20   Ilfracombe harbour and sheltered bay in 1830. The figure in the foreground with a telescope might be a Coastguard officer, patrolling the cliffs.

French smugglers were more likely to risk bringing cargoes to England. Soon there were reports that illicit goods were being run in on the local coasts again.

The Customs Board developed a sophisticated system of intelligence-gathering to help combat the upsurge in smuggling. In October 1816 it began to send Thomas Rodd, the Ilfracombe collector, information about vessels believed to be taking contraband to the Exmoor coast. The first tip-off had been received by the Board from Plymouth. It said that three craft of French rig, each of about 25 tons, had been seen recently west of Lundy looking as if they were heavily laden with spirits and waiting for dark to run in their cargoes. The ships originated from Morlaix in Brittany and it was thought they might have landed their contraband at Lee, or if not at some point further east on the Exmoor coast. The vessels had since returned to Roscoff to pick up another cargo, but could be expected to return. The Board also sent information received from the Scilly Isles stating that five boats from there had gone to Roscoff to collect contraband. The names of these boats were not known as they had been blacked out while they were in France. The Ilfracombe Customs officers were instructed to keep a close watch for them.

Thomas Rodd soon afterwards received another letter from the Board, this time with information received direct from Roscoff. The Board must have had a spy in France! A list of vessels loading contraband at the Brittany port was provided. It is interesting to note that included on the list was the French lugger *Adele*, a vessel that was to be seized by the Ilfracombe-based Revenue cutter *Harpy* in February 1819. The letter went on to instruct Rodd to be particularly on the lookout for a French schooner which was loading up to 400 kegs of geneva, each holding four gallons. The schooner was expected to sail 'for the neighbourhood of Minehead'. The letter advised that the vessel always had her contraband covered with 'hoops or other goods' and that she had run cargoes successfully to that part of the Exmoor coast in the previous winter. The collector was warned to be on his guard, for this schooner waited 'neither for dark nights nor favourable winds, depending entirely on her disguise'.

A number of seizures were made in the early years of peace. In 1817, as will be detailed in later chapters, contraband was seized at Ilfracombe harbour from both the Spanish brigantine *Feliz Restoración* and the Ilfracombe brigantine *Jane*. In October of the following year the Ilfracombe Revenue cutter *Harpy*, stopped and boarded the Norwegian ship *Kammerheye* off Hartland Point. The vessel's documents showed that she was bound from Santander in Spain to Bristol with a cargo of Spanish wool, and a quick search revealed that this was all intact. However, also on board were found a hogshead of brandy, five pipes of brandy (a pipe held the equivalent of two hogsheads), five bottles of brandy and eight hogsheads of wine, and none of these items were listed on the ship's manifest. The vessel and its cargo were seized and taken into Ilfracombe harbour. The Norwegian captain claimed that it had not been his intention to discharge the secondary cargo of brandy and wine until he returned to Norway, but the evidence suggested that in reality he had planned to unload it at some point on his passage up the Bristol Channel.

A seizure was also made while contraband was being moved inland. In 1818 a packman called John Whittle was stopped at Brendon and found to be carrying illicit goods on his packhorses. He was fined £10 for that offence and also sentenced to six months hard labour for assaulting the Excise officer who arrested him.

In February of the following year the *Harpy* went out from Ilfracombe on a cruise and came across the French sloop *Adele* off Trevose Head in Cornwall. The vessel hoisted all sail but was caught after a short chase. On board were found casks containing 571 gallons of brandy and 574 gallons of geneva. It was also discovered that several members of the *Adele's* crew were drunk after having sampled their cargo too freely. The incident caused quite a stir in Ilfracombe where both the vessel and French crew were detained for some time. The case against the smugglers seemed very strong, but eventually both the vessel and her crew were released. Needless to say the commander and crew of the *Harpy* were bitterly disappointed, for they had lost their chance of a substantial reward.

Other smuggling incidents were reported in the same period. In September 1820 William Cooke, a notorious local smuggler, successfully landed tubs of spirits at Lee, and on the following day ran more kegs ashore at Woody Bay (incidents to be described in Chapter 9). Also in that year the *Harpy* picked up five puncheons of rum at sea, two of them 'having taken in a great quantity of salt'. A similar find was made in July of the following year when two casks of salt-impregnated French red wine were picked up from the sea. These last two discoveries may have come about because smugglers were sinking contraband offshore to be picked up later. This was a technique used extensively by smugglers on the South Devon coast at this time, but does not seem to have been much practised on the Exmoor coast because of the large tidal range. If these kegs had been deliberately sunk, the smugglers could not have checked they were watertight!

In January 1822 another important step was taken in the efforts to suppress smuggling when it was announced that the Waterguard, the Customs cutters and the riding officers would be amalgamated into one body to be known as 'the Coast Guard'. The Customs Board was given over-all control, but a naval officer headed the body to improve discipline and efficiency. Previously, the different elements of the preventive service had sometimes pulled against each other, but the new integrated force was to prove a highly effective team in the battle to combat smuggling.

The local Coastguard forces achieved several notable successes. In November 1827 they discovered a very large hoard of contraband hidden in caves on a farm at Trentishoe (an incident described in Chapter 11). Enquiries revealed that for many years this farm had been the distribution centre for a gang of smugglers led by William Cooke. When the news of this important seizure reached Ilfracombe there was a riot, for local people realised the smugglers had suffered a crushing blow. At sea the biggest success came in 1831 when an Ilfracombe Revenue cutter seized the sloop *Lively* off Lundy with a cargo of brandy.

Victories were being won, but this did not prevent the Ilfracombe collector writing to the Customs Board in February 1831 to point out that more Coastguard officers were needed on this 'bold and dangerous coast' if smuggling was to be entirely stamped out. He was to be proved right. In January 1832 an Appledore vessel was seen landing a large cargo of brandy kegs on Lynmouth beach, and the three Coastguard men who tried to arrest the smugglers were totally outnumbered (the story is told in Chapter 12). Yet the preventive officers did manage to foil the landing and subsequently seized part of the cargo, so this could still be seen as a success.

Final victory for the preventive forces had still not been achieved, but by the early 1830s the Exmoor smugglers had suffered heavy losses and many of them were giving up the unequal battle. The end of the smuggling era was not far away.

8

William Matthews: A Courageous Commander

It is fashionable to glorify and romanticise the smuggler, but the story of William Matthews, a Revenue cutter commander, serves to remind us that sometimes it was the officers of the preventive services who were the real heroes. This is the story of his remarkable career with the Customs service, made even more interesting by the fact that the events described took place while the British people were engaged in a life or death struggle against Napoleon's forces.

William Matthews was sworn in as commander of the Revenue cutter *Shark* on 22 June 1804. For the next six years he took his instructions from the Barnstaple collector and patrolled the coast from Bridgwater right down to St Ives. What an eventful period this was! Seldom can a Revenue cutter have had such success. Matthews and his crew captured one smuggling vessel after another and in so doing faced danger, abuse and intrigue. Not all of this activity took place on the Exmoor coast, but it is important to record it, partly because the *Shark* operated out of Ilfracombe as well as Barnstaple, and also because his experiences illustrate so well the adventurous life of the commander of a Revenue cutter.

In appointing William Matthews the Customs Board had made an excellent choice, for he was a greatly experienced seaman with a detailed knowledge of the local coast and the trade that went on there. He had gone to sea at the tender age of ten and had risen to become a ship's master, commanding a variety of vessels operating in the Bristol Channel and the western approaches.

No sooner had Captain Matthews taken up his position as commander of the *Shark* than he went into action. On 18 July 1804 he came back over the Bar into Barnstaple Bay after a four-day cruise bringing with him the first of many seizures. The *Betsey* was a brand-new sloop from Fowey in Cornwall. It had 527 kegs of spirits plus a few cases of wine on board, and had been captured the previous evening at Bude Bay while in the act of landing a cargo obtained from Guernsey. Matthews realised that the tide was not sufficiently high to enable the *Betsey* to be brought to the custom-

21   Barnstaple Quay, c.1855. At the beginning of the century, Captain Matthews had received his instructions from the collector at this port.

house quay at Barnstaple so moored his prize at Appledore. Four Barnstaple tidesmen and some of the cutter's crew were instructed to guard the sloop and her contraband.

Matthews had little time to reflect on his success. The following morning the body of Joseph Perryman, one of the tidesmen on duty, was found floating near the *Betsey* with a neck wound. This incident triggered a major row between the Barnstaple and Bideford collectors and Matthews was inevitably sucked in. For a time his future as commander seemed in jeopardy.

Thomas Grant, the Bideford collector, informed the Customs Board that Perryman had met his death while trying to prevent part of the cargo being taken out of the *Betsey* by smugglers. In support he called attention to the coroner's inquest which had brought in a verdict of 'wilful murder by persons unknown'. Grant also claimed it was common knowledge 'on the streets' that, on the night the tidesman met his death, 103 kegs of spirits had been taken out of the *Betsey*, loaded into in a boat and taken up the Torridge estuary to Bideford. He also made the damaging assertion that the officers and crew on board the *Betsey* had been drinking the spirits and wine they were supposed to be guarding.

John Pitt, the Barnstaple collector, was furious. He claimed that his Bideford colleague was simply trying to discredit the Barnstaple officers in the hope that the Board would take responsibility for Appledore away from the port of Barnstaple and hand it instead to Bideford. Pitt claimed Perryman had not been murdered but had fallen overboard while drunk. He sent the Board a letter from the coroner saying that, despite the verdict of the jury, it was his view as a surgeon that Perryman had fallen overboard accidentally, been stunned and drowned. Pitt also claimed the locks to the hatches on the *Betsey* were intact and not a keg had been removed.

William Matthews' reputation and career hung in the balance. He wrote to the Customs Board saying that his character had been subjected to 'infamous attacks', but if it could be proved he had in any way neglected his duty he would 'cheerfully resign' his commission. Matthews admitted that on the night in question he had been absent from his cutter, but pointed out that the Barnstaple collector had given him permission to visit his wife and family at their house in Bideford. He also complained bitterly that soon afterwards the Bideford collector had gone with a constable and several Customs officers to this house and had ransacked it 'to the great alarm and annoyance of his wife and family'. They had failed to find a single keg of spirits. The Barnstaple collector added a note saying Matthews 'would not have met the treatment he has met with if he had not been such an active, faithful, diligent and enterprising officer'. Pitt may have been implying that Matthews was being picked on because he had been courageous enough to report a Mr Hackett, a local Excise officer, for 'actually aiding and assisting the smugglers' while they were unloading contraband out of the *Betsey* in Bude Bay.

After carrying out a detailed investigation into the *Betsey* incident, the Customs Board eventually came up with an inconclusive verdict, merely deciding that the accusation that Barnstaple Customs officers had removed contraband from the vessel had not been proved. The Board also felt there were no grounds for thinking that Perryman had been murdered. The Barnstaple and Bideford collectors were instructed to 'live in harmony with each other that the service may not suffer by their dissensions'.

Captain Matthews was desperate to have another opportunity to prove his worth but he had a problem, for when the *Shark* had arrived at Appledore she had been pronounced unfit to go back to sea. Her mast was damaged and she was said to be 'in a very leaky state'. A shipwright did

22   Woody Bay, c.1840. It was at this remote bay in 1804 that the Revenue cutter *Shark* seized a Bideford brigantine after surprising it in the act of unloading contraband.

some repairs but then found the *Shark's* planks were rotten. He caulked the cutter's upper parts but refused to pronounce her seaworthy. Matthews chose to ignore the shipwright's report and on 9 August ordered his vessel out to sea to patrol the Exmoor coast.

It soon seemed Matthews' recklessness might cost his crew their lives. In a matter of hours a 'hurricane' blew up. Matthews had the *Shark's* mainsail reefed and a storm jib put up, but still kept his cutter out searching for smugglers. As she approached Woody Bay, Matthews put his spyglass to his eye and spotted the Bideford brigantine *Margaretta* riding at anchor near the limekiln. She was well in to the shore where the cliffs gave some shelter from the offshore gale. Cargo was being discharged into three boats lying alongside.

Matthews ordered his mate George Need to take some of the crew in one of the *Shark's* longboats and investigate. On seeing the boat approaching, the three boats at once left the brigantine and tried to escape to the shore. The *Shark* pelted them with shot. When Need and his men boarded the brigantine they threw the hatches overboard and searched the hold. Hidden under a few tons of limestone they found a large quantity of contraband. They jumped back in the longboat and rowed to the shore where they arrested a number of men and took from them 45 ankers of spirits and 9 tons of salt.

In a letter Matthews described the 'deplorable' situation he and his crew faced as the gale blew even stronger. He sent some of his men to take charge of the *Margaretta*, it being by then 'quite dark and thick, dirty, rainy weather, blowing very heavy and no hatches on board the brigantine'. To preserve lives and vessels, he gave orders to run westwards before the storm. Heavy seas pounded the two vessels and both began to leak badly. The brigantine was also shipping water into her open hold. The weather grew worse and soon both vessels were in grave danger of sinking. Matthews wrote that had they not managed to reach Minehead both vessels 'must have perished'.

Once safely in port, the seized contraband was put under lock in the King's warehouse under the supervision of the Minehead collector. What a rich and varied assortment it was! It included one keg of rum, 9 kegs of wine, 150 kegs of geneva, 219 kegs of brandy, 693 bags of salt weighing in all about 35 tons, eight bales of tobacco and one bag of pepper. Not surprisingly, the Barnstaple collector was delighted to hear the news that a cutter under his control had achieved such a notable success so soon after facing fierce criticism from the Bideford collector. He wrote to the Customs Board expressing his 'highest terms of approbation' and saying that this success fully vindicated the trust placed in the commander and crew of the *Shark*.

The *Margaretta* was a Bideford vessel described as being 'of the type used in the limestone trade' and had been pretending to be engaged in lawful business, having the contraband concealed under limestone and unloading it near the Woody Bay limekiln. The fact that the brigantine came from Bideford is interesting, because during the dispute over the *Betsey*, the Barnstaple collector had accused his Bideford colleague of having recently allowed a limestone vessel to smuggle 144 kegs of spirits into Bideford. Could that vessel have been the *Margaretta* and could the Barnstaple officers have since been on the lookout for her, because they suspected the Bideford collector had a financial interest in her smuggling trips? We can only speculate.

A fortnight later Matthews took the *Shark* out on patrol, went down the Welsh coast as far as Milford Haven and then headed across to North Cornwall where he spotted a large lugger. Matthews had every sail put up and gave chase. Unfortunately, the lugger steadily pulled away and after three hours disappeared over the horizon. The commander was mortified for he felt sure she had at least 700 ankers of spirits on board. He believed the lugger was planning to run her contraband in on the Exmoor coast and headed back there for what proved a fruitless search.

While off Ilfracombe Matthews sent a letter to the Barnstaple collector complaining that his cutter creaked and groaned under canvas, and leaked water so badly that it was necessary to have the pumps going continually during a chase. He claimed that she was only capable of sailing at seven knots whereas most smuggling vessels could sail at least 12 knots:

> I plainly see if we cannot catch them napping we never shall by chasing … A British tar in His Majesty's service to be left in chase and laughed at would rather at a court martial receive sentence of death. Had we a craft that could sail, with 20 hands, my life but the duty that would be done would astonish you and many others. The *Shark* at present knows neither bribery nor corruption – our duty shall be done if life pays the tribute.

The Barnstaple collector then wrote a letter to the Customs Board enclosing estimates for essential repairs to the *Shark*, but firmly stating she was 'from her size, construction and manner of sailing incomplete to cope with the large smugglers which infest this Channel'. The Customs Board chose to ignore the suggestion that what was needed was a new Revenue cutter.

Matthews was not discouraged. On 10 March 1805 the commander had the satisfaction of reporting that he and his crew had captured the smuggling lugger *Dart* of Fowey, Cornwall, after using an unusual strategy. When this vessel was first spotted off the Exmoor coast the *Shark* was lying aground in Ilfracombe harbour, the tide being out, so the cutter could not immediately give chase. Matthews therefore sent out his two longboats. One of these longboats, commanded by Joseph Abbott, the acting mate, kept the *Dart* in sight but was unable to close on her. Eventually Abbott spotted the Barnstaple sloop *Goodwill* off Baggy Point, bound in ballast for Swansea, and commandeered her. The longboat was moored under the stern of the sloop, so the smugglers might not see her. Abbott then ordered the captain and mariners of the sloop between decks, and he and his five men took control of the vessel. For an hour and a half, they manoeuvred, trying to get to windward of the lugger without letting the smugglers realise they were being followed. Gradually they drew nearer the smuggling vessel. Then Abbott had his men rejoin the longboat. Suddenly they pulled out from behind the sloop and tried to close on the lugger, continually firing muskets at her. The *Dart* at once changed her tack and began heading away from the longboat in the direction of Clovelly. Fortunately, at this very moment the *Shark* appeared, having left Ilfracombe harbour as soon as the tide came in. The Customs cutter bore down upon the *Dart* and began firing. After a few shots the smugglers hauled down their sails, whereupon Captain Matthews went across in a boat and took possession of the lugger. He found she was laden with spirits, tobacco and pepper to the value of almost £4,000.

Other successes soon followed. In June 1805 Matthews took the *Shark* on what proved to be an eventful cruise along the North Cornwall coast. First the *Shark* sighted the *Union*, another Fowey smuggling lugger, and after following her for three days finally tracked her down after dark, close inshore off Bassett's Cove. Matthews ordered guns and muskets to be fired to prevent her escaping. The *Shark* closed with the lugger and grappled her. What they did not know was that a boat belonging to the *Dolphin*, a Revenue cutter based at St Ives, had approached the *Union* from the land side at the same time. It was only the shout of the *Dolphin's* mate 'A prize' that prevented the two crews opening fire on each other in the dark. Matthews was furious, but reluctantly called his men off to avoid confrontation. During the chase the crew of the *Union* had thrown most of her contraband overboard, but some 200 ankers of spirits were seized and Matthews wrote to the Board to request a share of the prize money for his crew for the part the *Shark* had played in the seizure.

The following day proved equally eventful. First, the crew of the *Shark* seized the *Lottery*, yet another Fowey smuggling lugger, north-west of Padstow, for hovering with a contraband cargo within eight leagues of the coast. Then Matthews spotted the *Heed*, a lugger from Mevagissey in Cornwall. He gave chase, lost her, but eventually found her off Newquay surrounded by small boats that were helping her take on ballast. Matthews realised the lugger must have just discharged her cargo, so he seized her. The commander was short-staffed and was obliged to remove his boarding party and take them to the shore in a longboat to search for contraband. Before leaving the *Heed* he warned Samuel Furze, the master, not to weigh anchor, but no sooner had the Revenue men left the smuggling vessel than she hoisted her sails and made off to the west.

Captain Matthews was very angry! He wrote a letter to the Customs Board pointing out that he was continually handicapped because his crew was far too small and as a result could man only one of the *Shark's* two longboats:

Although the *Shark* has been successful beyond expectation, as your Honours will perceive by the many valuable seizures she has made in the last twelve months, yet there is reason to suppose she would have been still more so if her complement of men would have enabled us to employ the boats more frequently, having only fourteen hands including myself, mate and boy. It is impossible to send out more than one boat at a time without disabling the cutter ...Having absolutely not had my clothes off for a fortnight together and, notwithstanding my exertions, I have had the mortification to see so many valuable seizures escape, a remarkable instance of which occurred in the case of the *Heed* lugger.

PORT OF BARNSTAPLE.

By order of the Honorable the Commissioners of His Majesty's Customs

ON Wednesday the 25th day of March, 1807, by ten o'clock in the forenoon, will be exposed to public SALE at the custom house in this port. the broken-up HULL and MATERIALS of the LOTTERY LUG-GER of Fowey, burthen 58 tons per register, seized by the Shark cruizer, William Ma-thews, commander, the 4th June 1805, and since con-demned in the exchequer.

—ALSO—

The broken-up HULL of the OLD SHARK CRUIZER, burthen about 70 tons, together with a *few* of her OLD STORES.

The above goods will be put up in *suitable* lots for the convenience of purchasers, and may be viewed two days preceding the sale on application at this office.

Custom house 27th February, 1807.

23 Advertisement in the *Exeter Flying Post* for an auction of the *Lottery*, a smuggling lugger captured by Captain Matthews, and of the old *Shark*, his former cutter. The vessels had been sawn in pieces to prevent them being purchased for use by smugglers.

The Customs Board ignored Matthews' plea for more hands, but when in February 1806 the *Shark* was condemned as unfit, they finally agreed to order a new cutter for him. While she was being built, the Board granted his request to use the lugger *Lottery* that he had recently seized, which he pointed out was 'quite new and supposed to be one of the fastest sailing vessels in the smuggling trade'. It is interesting to note that the new cutter was built at Mevagissey, which was where the smuggling lugger *Heed* was based. Three times Matthews went to the Cornish fishing village to inspect progress on the new cutter. The commander knew both the Dunn family, the owners of the *Heed*, and Samuel Furze, the master, a man who had several times threatened to have him murdered, but he never mentions seeing either them or the *Heed* while on these visits.

The Board later questioned the large expense account that Matthews had run up on his third visit to Mevagissey, when he went by land instead of in the *Lottery*. The commander took grave exception to this implied criticism. He wrote back to say he would have much preferred to travel by sea if the *Lottery* had not been in port having her stores checked. Matthews ended by pointing out the dangers he had faced by travelling by land across Cornwall: 'I was exposed to considerable peril in passing through the county of Cornwall, where the smugglers had constantly threatened to be revenged on me in consequence of the several seizures I had made from them.'

Commander Matthews took delivery of the new *Shark* in September 1806. The *Lottery* was no longer needed by the Customs service, so the original sentence of condemnation was carried out and she was sawn in three to prevent her being purchased for use by smugglers. The broken-up hull and materials were auctioned at Barnstaple and the broken-up hull of the old *Shark* was offered for sale at the same time.

On 30 September 1806 while out on his first cruise in the new *Shark*, Matthews came across the *Heed* off the coast of North Cornwall. This may have been no more than a remarkable piece of luck, but one wonders whether Matthews had used his visits to Mevagissey to collect information about the movements of the vessel that had escaped him just over a year earlier. For several hours he chased the deeply laden lugger, but eventually lost her. For several days the *Shark* plied up and down the coast, once spotting the *Heed* off Newquay but losing her again. Finally, on the morning of 6 October the *Shark* came across the lugger in thick fog, again off Newquay. Three shots were fired across the *Heed*'s bows, and then Matthews sent a party to board her. Unfortunately, there was no contraband on board, but they did find the logbook and in it was an entry showing the lugger had recently sailed from Guernsey. Matthews' description of the vessel's equipment is worth recording. He found 'a number of cooper's utensils, buckets, brass cocks and instruments for drawing off the spirits from the large casks into ankers by which three of the latter are filled at the same time'. The lugger was obviously fitted out to unload contraband quickly. Yet the holds held only ballast. When Matthews examined the material he realised it came from the beach at Harlyn Bay just to the west of Padstow.

There was not a moment to be lost! Matthews took six men and went in a longboat to the bay, this time leaving a large group of men guarding the *Heed*. There was no sign of life on the beach, but marks were found where kegs had been dragged across the sands and other proofs that a landing had been made within the last few hours. Matthews then took his men to search the village of Harlyn where they were met by a group of drunken and hostile men. The crowd increased in number as it grew dark until 40 men and horses, 'some with whips and some with bludgeons', surrounded the Customs men. Blows were struck, but Matthews was determined not to leave because he suspected that contraband was hidden away. He sent one man to fetch help from the Padstow custom-house and stood his ground. Matters worsened as the tide came in and some of his men were nearly drowned in the surf while hauling the longboat further up the beach. At first light Matthews and his men again searched the beach and in the sand dunes found a single keg, together with a small quantity of pepper and tobacco. By this time Matthews and his men were bruised, battered and exhausted. Two men had been injured while trying to rescue the boat from the rocks, one man had sustained a wound when he was attacked by a smuggler, and Matthews himself had an arm injured by a blow, which he said was 'of little consequence'. He wrote his report while lying sick and injured in his bunk and finished: 'I hope you will be perfectly satisfied we have done our duty as far as in our power.'

The *Heed* was an exceptional prize. She had been 'constantly employed in the smuggling trade' and was 'considered the fastest sailor from Guernsey'. Samuel Furze, the master, had been a smuggler all his life and had been heard to boast that no Revenue cruiser could catch the *Heed* out at sea. Yet twice previously she had been caught inshore, once by the *Shark* in 1805 and then earlier in 1806 by the frigate *Virginie* off the Irish coast with contraband on board. On the latter occasion the *Heed* had taken been taken into Cork and condemned, but somehow James Dunn, the owner, had managed to buy her back again.

The day after Matthews seized the *Heed*, Josiah Dunn, son of the owner, came on board the *Shark*. He told Matthews it was useless his trying to seize the lugger because he and his father had an agent in London by the name of Flowerdew who transacted all their business and would be able to have her released for a payment of £270. When this argument failed to shake Matthews' resolve, Dunn pointed out to Matthews that he would receive little or nothing in prize money by taking the lugger into port as on being condemned for a second time she would certainly be cut up. Matthews claimed that Dunn then offered him £50 to release the *Heed*, but he replied that even if Dunn offered him £5,050 he still intended to seize her.

As Josiah Dunn predicted, an agent acting for his family did contest the *Heed*'s seizure. In June 1807 the Customs Board's solicitor advised the Barnstaple collector that, although there could be no doubt that contraband had been landed at Harlyn Bay, he feared that the evidence of the *Heed*'s involvement was 'entirely presumptive' because not a single Cornishman could be found to give evidence against the smugglers. The

24 Wildersmouth, Ilfracombe, c.1830. This was one of several coves in or near Ilfracombe offering possibilities for illegal smuggling.

only grounds for her seizure therefore rested on a technicality. Here it should be explained that smuggling vessels had begun to imitate Revenue cutters in having long bowsprits, so that they could carry a greater spread of jib sails and thus sail faster, but in 1805 legislation had been passed banning the fitting of long bowsprits and certain jib sails to all but Revenue vessels and men-of-war. The *Heed* was not complying with this law because she had 'on board a jib topsail without any licence from the Admiralty'. The solicitor warned that because this sail was not set at the time of the seizure he doubted whether there were sufficient grounds to warrant the vessel being forfeited.

Matthews was very angry at the news. He wrote to the Customs Board and complained there was a campaign to have him removed from his post and that William Arthur, the notorious smuggler, was behind it. He also made his first reference to his poor health and finished by describing the danger he was in:

They are all smugglers in Cornwall and detest a Revenue officer ...I am sure my successes and strict attention to my duty has called forth the Guernsey merchants against me, if possible to get my dismissal from the service, nor will money be wanting if they can gain that point ... I am of the opinion that Arthur is not a stranger to their designs and that he has a hand with them. I am somewhat better than when you saw me last and I hope gaining strength every day. It would break my heart to be prevented from facing my enemies, particularly a set of men using every endeavour to take my life from me. This Furze in particular, how many times has he threatened me ... is it not in everybody's mouth? Is it not the cry down the whole coast that my life is in danger, go where I will?

Later that month, Captain Matthews, his mate, boatswain and a seaman were all called to London to give evidence in a case at the Court of the Exchequer to determine whether the *Heed* should be condemned or returned to her owners. Matthews took the jib sail with him on the coach from Barnstaple, still determined to beat the Dunns. Unfortunately, the Customs letter-books do not record the verdict.

Time after time Captain Matthews sailed out from Barnstaple or Ilfracombe to continue his campaign against the smugglers. In December 1806 he captured the cutter *Echo* near Padstow, in January 1807 the cutter *Rose* in Harlyn Bay with 326 ankers of spirits and then in May of that year the fine new cutter *Ida* with 517 large ankers of brandy and geneva on board. The *Ida* had been caught in the Irish Sea after a chase lasting 14 hours. The *Shark* had also assisted the Revenue cutter *Speedwell* in capturing the cutter *Valiant* near Boscastle in the previous month.

What is quite remarkable is that all four of the captured vessels hailed from Fowey, as had most of Matthews' earlier seizures. The commander must have been extremely unpopular there! Is it possible he had a spy in Fowey providing him with information about landing places and times?

In September 1807 Matthews and his crew had a miraculous escape. They had just been involved in two long sea chases, first after the cutter *Dart* and then after the lugger *Dover*, but both of these Guernsey-based vessels had managed to escape due to their greater speed. Matthews had reason to think the smugglers were planning to land their contraband at Bude Bay and had his longboats patrol there all night. When dawn came, the boats returned, having seen nothing. A gale then blew up and Matthews took the *Shark* to the more sheltered waters of Clovelly Roads, where he anchored. That night the wind veered to the north-west and blew with great violence, causing the cutter to drag her anchor and be in danger of drifting on to the shore. Matthews was obliged to slip the cable and hoist the storm sails to try and keep the cutter away from the shore. The storm increased and the *Shark* was blown towards Baggy Point. There seemed little hope. Matthews later described how the only course left to them was to try and cross the Bar, the sandbar at the entrance to Barnstaple Bay, before the tide was properly in:

> At six in the morn the winds veered round to north by west so that we could not weather away Baggy Point. Now there was no alternative but to run for the Bar, before the wind and sea which was tremendous. The foresail split, the sea making a free passage over us at this moment. Life was hanging by a very slender chance. I must confess for my own part I had very little hope. At twelve-past six it became necessary to clear the decks as much as possible, she being full of water from the quantity shipped, the ports all cut open before. We cleared the boats and should have hove the guns overboard, but could not get at them so as to unlash them from their places for the depth of water. In this state we were flying through the sea expecting every moment for her to strike, but at seven thanks to the good and gracious protector of mankind we found ourselves in safety over the Bar. We are now on Appledore beach and shall sail again as soon as the necessary ropes, sails and boats are replaced.

Matthews had managed to bring his vessel and crew to safety, but the Customs Board was soon faced with heavy bills for repairs to the vessel and the provision of new sails and a new longboat.

By 1808 Matthews had other problems to contend with. In August of that year he sent a letter to the Board explaining that his wife was seriously ill and requesting a month's leave of absence so that he could escort her to Bath to take the spa waters. He wrote:

In consequence of a very severe illness with which my wife has lately been afflicted, it has been deemed proper by the faculty for her to change the air and to try the use of the Bath waters. Therefore I request your Honours will grant me a month's leave of absence to accompany her, she being in so weak and languid a state as to be incapable of going alone and having no friend to whom I can safely confide her. I beg to assure your Honours nothing but the most singular necessity has impelled me to make this application, having never before been absent a day for upwards of the last three years I have been in the service.

It seems that permission was granted and Matthews went off with his wife to Bath. We are not told if the spa waters proved beneficial.

There are no records of seizures by the *Shark* in 1809, the reason being that for much of that year she was withdrawn from Customs service at Barnstaple to go on active duty with the ill-fated Walcheren expedition, Britain's ill-fated strike against Napoleon's forces at Antwerp. The *Shark* was one of a number of Customs cutters that acted as marker boats on the Schelde, guiding in the British transports carrying the army that was to attack Flushing and Antwerp. Yet even while serving the Royal Navy on the Continent, Matthews still carried on his personal war against smugglers. He noted that the crews of the cutter *Stag* of Rye, and the luggers *Dart* of Folkestone and *Ox* of Deal, all of which were being employed by the Navy to act as buoy vessels marking difficult channels, were spending much of their time buying contraband. Matthews saw boats from these vessels go to the shore, load up with tea, tobacco and tubs of spirits, and then head out towards the North Sea where vessels from England were waiting a mile out to sea to meet them. He informed his commanding officer, but was told that chasing smugglers was not a priority and nothing could be done unless the boats were caught out at sea with the contraband on board.

In October 1809 Captain Matthews brought the *Shark* back to England only to learn that his wife was gravely ill. She was in London having treatment for 'mental derangement'. Matthews was given leave of absence. He rushed to see her, only to find her condition had worsened. They set off to travel home to Devon but sadly had only reached Bagshot, in Surrey, when she died.

By this time Matthews was himself a sick man, exhausted after his arduous service in Holland, distressed at the loss of his wife and suffering great 'anxiety and trouble of mind'. On 20 November he rejoined the *Shark* at Appledore, but his health suffered a 'relapse' and on 7 December he was obliged to ask for sick leave. James Crockford, the mate, had to take the Revenue cutter out on patrol in his place. Matthews rejoined his ship on 17 January 1810 but after taking the *Shark* out into the Bristol Channel on duty for 19 days he returned to Ilfracombe on 9 February 'in a weak and very unfit state' and had to be taken to his home in a chaise. Once again he was obliged to request sickness leave. The physician who examined him declared 'the disease was in his head and occasionally affected the intellect' and that 'it would be highly imprudent for him to proceed to sea until relieved from the malady'. John Pitt, the Barnstaple collector, wrote to the Board in Matthews' support saying he believed the commander's anxiety to return to his ship had 'augmented his complaint'.

While still confined to his bed, Matthews received a body blow. At the beginning of March 1810 the Customs Commissioners advised him they were going to 'discontinue' the *Shark* in July. The cutter's mate and most of the crew were to be reassigned to serve on preventive boats at Port Isaac, Clovelly and Porlock, but there was no mention of a new role for the commander. This move was prompted in part by the national reorganisation of the Customs service then taking place, which led to the Preventive Waterguard coming into being in July. Yet there also seems to have been a hidden agenda, for it soon it became clear that while the commander and crew were being discharged from the *Shark*, the cutter was to continue in service. The Board instructed Matthews that in July the *Shark* was to be moved from Barnstaple to Ilfracombe and put under the control of the collector there. Furthermore, the captain and crew of the lugger *Alarm*, then in the service of the Customs at Exeter, were to be sent up to Ilfracombe to replace Matthews and his crew on the cutter. The *Shark* would then be renamed the *Alarm*. It seems the Board had forgotten the sterling service rendered by the existing commander and crew of the *Shark* and for some reason had decided to have a clean sweep.

At least it seemed that Captain Matthews was to be financially provided for. His salary was paid during the 150 days he was sick between October

1809 and May 1810. He then recovered sufficiently to take command of his cutter again. On 21 July the commander delivered her to Ilfracombe where he parted with the *Shark* and her crew. The Board advised him he would receive what was then a very substantial salary of £125 per annum 'unless and until' he was again employed by the Customs. He must have wondered what the future held for him.

Matthews was now without a ship, but that did not prevent him offering his services to the Customs on a voluntary basis. In September 1810 he wrote to the Board saying that 'since being discontinued' he had kept himself 'constantly employed' travelling and making 'every minute enquiry possible' to gather intelligence about contraband-running. His letter provided a wealth of useful information on smuggling, but reached the conclusion that large-scale contraband runs had totally ceased on the coast from Land's End to Bristol. Matthews perhaps hoped the Board would realise that this was at least in part due to all the seizures that he had made over the last six years. He finished by expressing the hope that his information was of some use to the service that he was so proud to serve.

Sadly, this was not to be a story with a happy ending. A letter received in July from the collector at Padstow may first have aroused the Board's suspicions. He complained that Captain Matthews had delivered to him for harbour duty a 25-foot boat instead of the 18-foot boat belonging to the *Shark* that the commander had been instructed to send. The Board may have been uneasy that something was not as it should be, for soon afterwards William Earnshaw, a Surveyor-General for the Customs, was sent to the Barnstaple custom-house to investigate.

Earnshaw's enquiry gradually expanded until it unearthed a whole catalogue of misdemeanours committed by John Pitt, the Barnstaple collector. For example, in 1787 instead of destroying 1,043 ankers of seized spirits as instructed, he had kept 49 for the use of himself and his officers while the remainder he had sold for his own profit. Even more seriously, he had tricked Matthews into signing blank receipts, with the result that Pitt had pocketed most of the prize money to which the commander and crew of the *Shark* were entitled for the seizures they had made. Three receipts alone showed Matthews being paid a total of £3,620. 5s 8d in prize money when in fact he had received not a penny. In December 1811 the collector was dismissed. So too was John Oram, comptroller at Barnstaple, for 'disobedience to his instructions to be a complete check upon the collector in every part of his duty'.

Unfortunately for Matthews, it was a minor irregularity over one of the

Shark's boats that had triggered the enquiry and Earnshaw found evidence to show that Matthews had not been honest in the matter. When back in 1804 the commander had seized the *Betsey*, he had decided to keep her boat for use with the *Shark*. The reason for this is not clear, but possibly one of the *Shark's* official boats had been lost through negligence and this boat was needed to replace her. In any event, Matthews had not sought the Board's permission to keep the *Betsey's* boat. One small misdemeanour had led to another. When, in the following year, the *Betsey* and her boat had been condemned for having been involved in smuggling and Matthews had been instructed to hand over the boat to the Navy, he had given up the boat from another of his seizures, the *Lottery*. Then when the *Lottery* and her boat had been ordered to be destroyed for being involved in smuggling, Matthews had substituted for the *Lottery's* boat an old one he had bought for only 10 shillings and that had been broken up instead. So, when in 1810 Matthews had been ordered to send one of the *Shark's* boats to Padstow, it seems he may well have tried unsuccessfully to substitute the one that formerly belonged to the *Betsey*. Certainly he had subsequently sold this boat and kept for himself the relatively small sum it realised. One cannot condone these offences, but they were relatively small ones when set in the context of the magnificent service Matthews had given, so the Board's letter to the acting collector at Barnstaple in December 1811 must have come as a terrible shock:

> We find him guilty and deem him an unfit person to be any longer continued in the service of the Revenue and have dismissed him there-from and direct his allowance to be discontinued from the date hereof and you are to call in his commission and instructions and transmit the same hither cancelled.

Captain Matthews had been drummed out of the service and left without an income. The punishment seems extremely harsh in the circumstances. The fact that the commander had not realised he had not been paid most of the prize money owing to him should have been evidence enough that he had not been trying to profit at the Crown's expense. Logic should have said that here was an exceptional officer who had occasionally employed slightly unorthodox methods, but as a result had been remarkably successful.

The Board had obviously paid little attention to a letter sent them in the previous year by Captain Matthews when first he realised that his ship was to be taken away from him. He had written:

I have executed the duty entrusted to me with fidelity and energy and by my unremitting exertions have contributed in a vast measure to the annihilation of smuggling from the whole line of coast this side of the Land's End of England.

This was not an exaggeration. In fact the Customs service owed him an enormous debt for his work. He had made an unprecedented number of seizures and had done more than any other man to rid the Bristol Channel and its western approaches of smugglers.

Captain Matthews' illustrious career as commander of the *Shark* thus ended in disgrace. It was a hard end for a man who had given such valiant service. He had faced danger, violence, intimidation and the hatred of the smuggling gangs, but had shown himself to be a man of courage and a loyal officer.

9

William Cooke: A Wily Smuggler

Smugglers are shadowy figures. We know they existed, but it is extremely difficult to find hard evidence about them. Only rarely were they caught and even then they often managed to convince the authorities that they were simply innocent bystanders. William Cooke was one such man. It seems he frequently ran in cargoes on the Exmoor coast, but we have to rely on a few isolated incidents to try to piece together an impression of the man and his methods of operation.

It was in 1817 that Cooke first came to notice. He was master of the Ilfracombe brigantine *Jane*, which on 2 July called at Ilfracombe harbour. The ship was bound from Oporto in Portugal to Bristol with a cargo of boxes of lemons and hogsheads of wine. The wind was favourable for her to sail up the Bristol Channel and there seemed no good reason why she should make this unscheduled stop. William Cooke claimed he had come in because his vessel was 'leaky', but this seems to have been an excuse. The Excise cruiser *Resolution* happened to be in the harbour and Lieutenant William Price, her second officer, had his suspicions aroused when he saw the crew made no effort to pump any water out of the *Jane* once she anchored.

That evening Lieutenant Price kept watch with Robert Hulland, the Ilfracombe comptroller. Just after dusk they saw a pilot boat go out to the *Jane*. A short time later it returned. Three members of the *Jane's* crew left the boat and went up the steps to the quay. The two officers and several of their men stepped out of the shadows and arrested them. The three sailors were found to be carrying two hampers containing 81 bottles of wine. They were placed in custody on the *Resolution* and the seized contraband was securely stored in the King's warehouse under the Excise lock. Lieutenant Price then went out to the *Jane* in a boat. On rummaging the vessel he found a further 106 bottles of wine, nine bottles of shrub (made from spirits and sweetened fruit juice), two quarts of geneva and three quarts of rum, secreted in different parts of the ship and obviously intended to be smuggled. James Lister, the commander of the *Resolution*, then seized the vessel because contraband had been concealed on board.

William Cooke was now in serious trouble and things became much worse when John Anthony, one of the three sailors involved, went before a Justice of the Peace and made a sworn statement in which he said that Cooke had ordered him to take the hampers on shore. If the Customs Board believed that the master of the *Jane* had instigated the smuggling, then the ship would certainly be forfeit and Cooke would be ruined.

Cooke therefore petitioned the Customs Commissioners for the release of his brigantine, putting forward a number of reasons why he was entirely blameless in the matter. First, he said that Anthony was a 'foreigner' and thus could not be relied on. He also suggested that the comptroller had persuaded Anthony to falsely accuse him of organising the smuggling, on the understanding that Anthony would not be prosecuted for having assaulted the comptroller during the arrest. Cooke went on to make the remarkable claim that most of the 187 bottles of wine had been intended for his personal consumption and that he had fully intended to drink them before reaching England, but the passage had been quicker than expected. He said it was the first time he had made a voyage of this nature and therefore was ignorant of the fact that it was illegal to import wine in bottles. He also asserted it had been his intention to pay the duty on any bottles still remaining when he reached Bristol. Most importantly, Cooke stated that during the 12 years he had been master of a vessel he had never before 'even been suspected of smuggling'. He finished by pleading with the Commissioners to release his vessel and allow him to complete his voyage to Bristol, as actions were being instituted against him by merchants there who had been expecting their lemons and wine to arrive.

William Cooke also prevailed on Richard Frizell, the minister of an llfracombe church, together with Nathaniel Lee and Nathaniel Vye, churchwardens, to testify that he was well known to them and was 'an honest, sober and industrious man' who, to the best of their knowledge, had never before been involved in smuggling. There seems a certain irony that these churchmen should be pronouncing Cooke to be a 'sober' citizen while he was claiming that he had planned to drink up to 187 bottles of wine on the voyage back from Portugal!

The Commissioners seem to have been persuaded by Cooke's arguments, for on 15 July they ordered the release of the *Jane*. The brigantine at once set sail for Bristol with her cargo. Yet the three unfortunate members of her crew who had been caught smuggling were sent to Plymouth and impressed into the Royal Navy, despite the fact that they still claimed they had only been obeying their master's orders.

Cooke was still not satisfied. On 16 July he had the audacity to petition the Commissioners again, thanking them for releasing the vessel but asking that he might have back all the wine and spirits seized on board. He again said that he would have largely consumed it all on the passage from Portugal had the passage back to England not been unusually quick, only ten days. Sadly, Cooke seemed indifferent to the fate of three of his men. He gave the impression of being shocked to find they had been involved in smuggling, and expressed his satisfaction that the Navy had impressed them, saying it was 'merited punishment'. He finished by again claiming he was in no way involved and said he hoped that 'a character of twelve years as a ship master unimpeached' would exonerate him from suspicion. Indeed he put forward such convincing arguments that one can understand why he might have been believed.

Yet in 1820 William Cooke was again implicated in smuggling, this time on a much larger scale. On 20 September the Barnstaple collector wrote to inform the Board that he had been making 'strict and diligent' enquiries after receiving a report that smuggling had been taking place organised 'by some desperate character who has lately returned from the Continent'. The

25   The sheltered cove at Lee, near Ilfracombe, c.1855. William Cooke is known to have smuggled a cargo of spirits in here in 1820.

collector said he had eventually discovered from various sources that the person in question was Cooke, a person whose family resided in Ilfracombe, and that he had indeed run in very large quantities of contraband. He went on to say that Cooke had 'landed 300 tubs, each containing five gallons, of Hollands gin and French brandy at Lee', west of Ilfracombe, which was 'successfully and immediately carried off into the interior'. Furthermore, the following day the remainder of the cargo 'consisting of upwards of 300 more tubs of the same spirits' had been landed at Woody Bay 'with equal facility and security'. The Barnstaple collector finished by saying he felt it his duty to send this account, even though he assumed 'a more particular report' would already have been made by the Ilfracombe collector, as the stretch of coast where the two landings had taken place was within that officer's area of responsibility. One can almost detect the Barnstaple official feeling a smug satisfaction in pointing out that the smuggler had been able to operate on his neighbour's territory without being detected.

In fact the Ilfracombe collector had been totally unaware that landings of contraband had taken place on his coast until the Board wrote to him asking for his observations. He then investigated and found himself in the embarrassing position of having to write back to confirm that Cooke had indeed smuggled in a cargo of spirits. The collector also reported that the crew of the preventive boat stationed at Clovelly had found one keg buried in the shingle on the beach at Lee. He said his officers had diligently searched to see if they could find where the remainder of the contraband was hidden but without success. Furthermore, in the absence of any riding officers on this stretch of coast, the crew of the Revenue cruiser *Harpy* had patrolled the area where the two landings had taken place but had not come across any of the smugglers. Cooke and his men seemed to have totally outwitted the Customs officers.

The Customs officers never managed to arrest and prosecute Cooke for smuggling. In the next chapter it will be shown that he was in fact the son-in-law of Thomas Rodd, the Ilfracombe collector, and there were suggestions that his influential relative was protecting him.

10

Thomas Rodd: A Suspect Collector

Customs collectors carried a heavy burden of responsibility. They were in overall charge of collecting duties and coordinating anti-smuggling measures at a port. This chapter considers a brief period in the life on an Ilfracombe collector that highlights some of the conflicts involved in this work.

Thomas Rodd had been appointed collector at Ilfracombe in February 1804, so he was an experienced official by 1817, the year that it was discovered contraband was being run ashore from two vessels in his harbour. The incidents caused him grave embarrassment, for there were accusations that smuggling was taking place under his nose and he was doing little or nothing to prevent it.

The *Feliz Restoración* entered Ilfracombe harbour in May of that year. Shortly afterwards, Henry Symonds, a crew member, went to William Rock, the tide surveyor, and informed him he had seen a quantity of brandy being smuggled ashore out of the schooner. The officer searched properties all along the harbourside, but not a single cask was found. Yet clearly contraband had been brought ashore, for the tide surveyor reported to the Customs Board that it was 'notoriously believed' that goods had been illegally landed and that the vessel was 'so very apparently lighter on the water than when she arrived at this port'. What is more, information was received that brandy from the vessel was being offered for sale in Barnstaple.

Rumours abounded. Thomas Rodd and his officers were being ridiculed and eventually the collector felt obliged to take action. Enquiries were made and Elizabeth Marshall, a local resident, was prevailed upon to make a sworn statement that Genova Gonay, the master, had smuggled ashore and given her ten quarts of brandy and rum, together with a quantity of coffee, sugar, calico and handkerchiefs. When Rodd reported this to the Board he was instructed to detain both the vessel and its cargo.

It is interesting here to note that Fanny Burney, the novelist, arrived in Ilfracombe soon afterwards on a visit, and described seeing this Spanish ship in the harbour. Her sympathies seemed to lie with the master of the seized ship who had been obliged to dismiss all his crew, except for his

26 Ilfracombe harbour, c.1830. Contraband was often smuggled ashore from vessels moored in the harbour.

physician, servant, cook and boy. She was told he was on parole until his trial, and was at liberty to go where he chose, but did not want to leave his vessel. The captain was obviously attracting the attention and sympathy of the visitors and residents alike. She wrote: 'He is a good-looking man, and, while not condemned, all are willing to take his word.'

The owners of the *Feliz Restoración* were determined to have their ship released. Lawyers were hired and they tried to destroy the credibility of the two witnesses to the smuggling. First they claimed Henry Symonds was a 'felon'. Then from the Ilfracombe minister and churchwardens they obtained a certificate stating Elizabeth Marshall was a 'common prostitute'. The Customs Board must have been convinced by their arguments, for on 27 July the collector was instructed to release the vessel on payment by the owners of £10 to cover the costs of those who had seized her. Presumably any charges against the master were dropped at the same time. After being held for over two months, the Spanish ship finally sailed away, much higher in the water than when she had come in. The incident had gravely damaged Thomas Rodd's reputation in the port.

On 2 July, in the middle of this controversy, William Cooke brought the *Jane* into Ilfracombe harbour. In Chapter 9 it was explained that Robert

Hulland, the comptroller, and William Price, lieutenant on the Excise cutter *Resolution*, discovered smuggling taking place and detained three members of the crew. Here it is worth pointing out that although Thomas Rodd was in charge of preventive measures at the port, he did not instigate the arrest of the smugglers, nor did he take any part in the subsequent seizure of the vessel. It was James Lister, commander of the *Resolution*, who held the seized wine and spirits 'under the Excise lock'. It was also Lister who seized the *Jane*, much to the collector's annoyance, as he felt he should have been consulted. In fact, some felt the collector was totally opposed to the actions taken.

After only 13 days the Customs Board sent instructions that the *Jane* was to be released and only the wine seized was to be retained. This might have been expected to be the end of the affair but far from it! The freeing of the ship seems to have intensely angered both the comptroller and the commander of the *Resolution* for they both suspected the collector had colluded with the smugglers. They may also have felt frustrated because they would have received a share of the reward if the *Jane* had been condemned and auctioned off.

By August the comptroller was no longer prepared to acquiesce in what he saw as the collector's deceit. So when Rodd wrote a letter to the Board stating that he did 'not know anything incorrect' in Cooke's claim that the wine had all been found hidden in lockers on the *Jane*, Hulland refused to sign it. This was unprecedented, for all official port correspondence had to be signed by both the collector and the comptroller. Instead the comptroller wrote a separate letter to the Board pointing out that in addition to the wine found on board the *Jane*, two hampers of wine were seized while actually being run ashore by members of the crew. The comptroller seems to have been reminding the Board that smuggling had taken place and that the collector was glossing over it.

Worse was to follow. The commander of the *Resolution* wrote a letter to the Board complaining that he had been subjected to a 'great deal of personal abuse' from the collector for seizing the *Jane* and the wine. As if that was not sufficient, Lister then went on to claim that the brigantine actually belonged to Rodd's relatives and that Rodd was a part-owner. These were serious allegations, for if true they meant the collector had a personal interest in having both vessel and wine freed from seizure. This was not all! Captain Lister also stated that Rodd was actually William Cooke's father-in-law and implied that the collector had turned a blind-eye when Cooke had contraband run in. Lister finished by asking the Board to stop the collector trying to 'vindicate the cause of persons found defrauding the revenue'.

Rodd was asked by the Board to reply to these allegations.This is part of what the collector had to say about the commander of the Excise cutter:

> He insulted me in the grossest manner in the open street as well as in the custom-house and even went so far as to declare that it was my age protected me from being thrashed by him. He says I abused him for seizing the wine, that the vessel is commanded by my son-in-law, and it appears very evident that I am indirectly a part owner of her. My son-in-law certainly does command her and is a part owner, but that would not in the least degree bias my conduct in respect of my duty to the Government. As for being a part owner, I am not nor never was in any manner interested in her and I call on him to prove what he has written … I request your Honours to call on Mr Lister to prove what he says respecting my vindicating the conduct of persons found smuggling.

This was indeed a remarkable letter! On the one hand it shows that two senior officers had been involved in public slanging-matches. More importantly, the collector had been obliged to admit that Cooke was indeed his son-in-law.

Later in his letter Rodd hit back hard by claiming that the commander's only motive in seizing the *Jane* had been to obtain a substantial share of the prize money and that, when the Board ordered her release, Lister's feelings were 'hurted and his temper he could not command'.

The situation was tense. The Board had to investigate. They asked the comptroller to provide his view of the events. This was what Hulland wrote:

> I beg leave to acquaint your Honours that Captain Lister came to the custom-house to call the collector to an account for the scurrilous language he made use of to him in the public street, and that Captain Lister told him in my presence that it was his age protected him. In consequence the collector and Captain Lister had high words and I must say that the collector used language much unbecoming in a gentleman by calling Mr Lister a blackguard. As to the collector having any part of the vessel in question I do not know, only that his son Thomas had a part in the said vessel, who has been dead many years, and who that part belongs to at present does not appear in the registry book kept in this office.

The comment about the registry book was particularly damaging. First, it was the collector's job to ensure that this book, listing all vessels officially registered at the port, was kept up to date. Secondly, any suggestion that he had failed to register an interest held by a member of his family in a port under his control had to be taken seriously.

Thomas Rodd wrote a letter of reply to these allegations. Significantly, he made no mention of the registry book, but asserted it was Captain Lister who had used scurrilous language. Rodd's main argument was that Hulland was 'in combination with Captain Lister' as they had hoped to profit from the seizures they had made. He finished by claiming to have always 'discharged the duty of the office' he held 'in a faithful manner'.

The Board was not satisfied and made further enquiries. Rodd was eventually asked to swear an affidavit stating he had no interest in the brigantine *Jane*. This he did, though it is worth pointing out that one of his sons admitted in another affidavit to holding a one-eighth share in the vessel. The outcome was surprising. Thomas Rodd was allowed to continue in his post as collector despite all the concerns raised by the comptroller and the captain. Perhaps the Board gave him the benefit of the doubt.

Both the *Feliz Restoración* and the *Jane* were released from custody and sailed away, but a question mark was left against the name of the Ilfracombe collector. Had Thomas Rodd actually been involved in contraband-running? Certainly in this period it was not uncommon to find collectors colluding with smugglers. This was in part due to the relatively low salaries they received, but it was also caused by their jealousy of the commanders of both the Customs and Excise cutters who made far more seizures than they did and thus received much more reward money. In Thomas Rodd's case insufficient evidence has survived to make a conclusive assessment. However, he seems to have been lucky to escape dismissal either for incompetence or for actually conniving at smuggling.

So Rodd kept his post and salary of £200 per annum. Not until 1824, at the age of 70, did he retire and then only due to an asthmatic condition and a 'shattered constitution'. The irony was that when the Board carried out its customary enquiries so as to decide whether he qualified for the allowance due to a superannuated officer, it was Robert Hulland, his vigilant comptroller, who made a statement that Rodd had always served the Customs 'with diligence and fidelity'.

11

Trentishoe: A Lawless Incident

In the early nineteenth century Trentishoe was a tiny farming hamlet tucked away in an isolated valley far from any road. Yet it was here that Revenue officers made the largest inland seizure ever recorded on Exmoor. This in turn triggered rioting in the normally peaceful port of Ilfracombe, demonstrating the strong local support for smugglers.

In late November 1827 a large cargo of contraband was brought in at Heddon's Mouth, probably in a small French vessel. Thomas Martin, the Lynmouth riding officer, heard about this run and began to make enquiries. On 3 December he and five Preventive Waterguard boatmen from the Ilfracombe coastguard station raided a farm belonging to John Hoyles at Trentishoe. After a 'laborious' search of the dwelling house and out buildings, they found the entrance to a man-made cave in a stable, concealed under straw. In the underground chamber were hidden 38 tubs of foreign spirits.

After making the discovery the officers questioned Hoyles closely. The farmer claimed there was nothing further hidden on his farm, but reports described him as being 'greatly agitated, confused and seized with tremors'. Hoyles's wife then asked if her husband could go into the farmhouse to change his clothes before being taken to the custom-house in Ilfracombe. The officers agreed, but after waiting over ten minutes they went inside and found he had escaped through a back window.

John Hoyles was never captured and it was believed he fled the country. It seems truly astonishing that the farmer had not been better guarded. Had the Revenue officers been concentrating on the seizure they had just made, which would bring them a much bigger reward than capturing a single smuggler? Or had they struck a secret deal with the farmer to give him his freedom? It is impossible to tell, but this is another instance of a smuggler escaping justice.

The following day the Revenue officers resumed their painstaking search of the farm. Eventually they came to a barn and here Hoyles's wife became agitated, striking out at them and doing all in her power to prevent them rummaging properly. The officers persisted and after moving piles of corn

27   The lower Heddon valley, 1855. In earlier times contraband landed at Heddon's Mouth would have been carried along this lonely valley.

they discovered the entrance to another cave, which appeared to have been recently 'enlarged and repaired for the reception of goods'. In it they found a further 174 tubs of foreign spirits. The search continued and two days later in a stable at the other side of the farm the officers found a third cave, this time containing 50 tubs of foreign spirits, four casks of wine, two cases of cordials and one case of preserved fruits. Put together the contents of the three caves represented a major seizure, consisting of 974 gallons of brandy, 66 gallons of geneva, 4 gallons of cherry brandy, 26 gallons of French wine, 41 bottles of cordials and 24 bottles of foreign preserves.

Three of the Waterguard boatmen and a constable at once set off to escort seven cartloads of the contraband on the ten-mile journey over poor roads to Ilfracombe. On reaching the port the seized goods were deposited at the custom-house and Warren Williams, the chief boatman, went to make a report to Lieutenant McKenzie, his commanding officer. The lieutenant at once gave orders that the boatmen and the constable were to collect up the carts and their drivers and go straight back to Trentishoe to see if they could find any further caches of contraband.

By this time it was about nine o' clock in the evening and the officers could not have relished the prospect of turning out again on a dark winter's night to travel back to Trentishoe. Nevertheless they went straight to the Exeter Inn where they knew the carters were having a drink. As they were about to set off from the inn, a hostile crowd of some 300 people gathered outside. Eyewitnesses later stated that a man carrying an 'effigy' led the mob but their reports do not explain who or what the figure represented. The atmosphere became tense and intimidating, with the crowd screaming threats and abuse. The carters refused point blank to go outside, saying they feared being murdered. The officers and constable must have been equally frightened, but they bravely went out onto the street, to go back to their commanding officer and seek further instructions. They were set upon by some of the crowd, who hurled rocks at them and beat them with sticks and staves. Waving his hat and urging on the mob was Thomas Hoyles, a relative of John Hoyles and himself a Trentishoe farmer. Warren Williams, the chief boatman, drew his sword, but it was only with great difficulty that he and his men managed to make their way back to Lieutenant McKenzie's house. Later that night McKenzie went with his officers to seek the 'protection' of Mr Lee, a magistrate, who accompanied the officers as they made their way out of Ilfracombe by a back way to avoid the fury of the mob.

A few days later Mr Andrews, the Inspector-General of Coastguards, sent a long report of the incident to his headquarters in which he praised the exemplary behaviour of the officers involved in making the seizure. First, he commended the 'steadiness, perseverance and sobriety' of Thomas Martin, the riding officer who had first gleaned information suggesting that contraband was hidden at the Trentishoe farm. Then he praised the bravery and devotion to duty of the chief boatman and crew of the Ilfracombe coastguard station who 'were never out of their clothes for six days and nights'. He also had a word for Lieutenant McKenzie, who 'was on the sick list' but rose from his bed to take charge when the mob threatened his men.

The Inspector-General also stated that the recent events had 'caused a great sensation in this part of the country'. Indeed they had and the Inspector General gave the reason in his letter when he wrote: 'John Hoyles is a near relation of Cooke, the most notorious smuggler in this part of the country.' He went on to explain that the farm had been the 'depot' for Cooke's entire operation for many years. No wonder there was such a stir! Exmoor's major smuggling operation had at last been smashed.

The Ilfracombe riot had certainly shown that the smugglers still commanded considerable support among the local populace. Maybe some

28 Trentishoe in 1908. In 1827 Revenue officers searched a farm in this tiny hamlet and found 262 tubs of foreign spirits hidden in man-made caves.

of the rioters also sensed that the smuggling era was gradually coming to an end and were expressing their anger that the days when they could buy duty-free spirits and tobacco were almost over.

12

Smugglers Surprised at Lynmouth

In January 1832 a large smuggling run was foiled. Watching out over the sea at Ilfracombe, the Coastguard men saw a small sailing ship going up the Bristol Channel. For some reason their suspicions were aroused. They rode along the coast following the vessel until it anchored a short distance from Lynmouth, as if waiting for the tide. Someone hailed her and was told that she was laden with china clay and bound for Gloucester. Not convinced, the officers watched from a vantage-point on the cliffs.

Part-way through the night, the three Coastguard men saw a number of farmers with packhorses gathering on the beach. Lights flashed and a boat came to the shore laden with over 30 kegs of brandy. The tubs were lifted out of the boats and the farmers began loading them onto their horses. At

29   Fishermen at Lynmouth, c.1825. The fishing industry had been badly hit by the disappearance of the herring shoals at the end of the eighteenth century.

30   The isolated village of Lynmouth, c.1828. In 1832 Revenue officers foiled an attempt to land a large quantity of foreign spirits here.

this point the preventive men hurried down and surprised the smugglers. They seized the spirits and three of the horses, though in the confusion both the sailors and farmers escaped. The Coastguard men then decided that they needed reinforcements to help guard the contraband. So, while two of the officers stood guard over the kegs, the third mounted one of the packhorses and rode off to Porlock to seek help.

This proved unwise, for no sooner had he left than a second boat came to the shore and this too began to unload kegs of brandy. When the crew of this boat realised there were two preventive men on the beach, they attacked them and 'severely beat them'. The farmers then emerged out of the shadows, reclaimed their two remaining packhorses and some of the kegs and disappeared into the night. The crew rowed back to their vessel, leaving the injured Coastguard men and most of the brandy lying on the beach.

The vessel immediately set sail, putting in at Appledore, where she landed the remainder of her cargo before sailing out to sea. Customs officers almost immediately captured 22 kegs of brandy at Appledore, while

Excise officers subsequently recovered 16 others, which had been carried up the Taw estuary in a boat and hidden in a house in the parish of Heanton.

The *North Devon Journal* carried a report of this smuggling run in which it stated that the vessel was a large pleasure yacht and was the 'property of a gentleman of Appledore'. Yet there was no subsequent report of this man being convicted of smuggling. Perhaps he had influence with the local magistrates and was able to escape prosecution.

The Ilfracombe collector's records show that 40 tubs of spirits were seized at Lynmouth. This figure is interesting because the *North Devon Journal* states that 64 kegs were seized. One wonders why there was such a large discrepancy in the figures! The records also show that shortly afterwards the riding officer seized a further horse laden with 4 tubs of brandy in the parish of Countisbury. Two farm labourers who had been escorting the horse claimed not to know how the goods had been landed or indeed who owned the horse. They said they had been employed merely to pick up the kegs at

31   Packhorses at Lynmouth, c.1855. In earlier times, animals such as these had carried contraband up to Lynton and the moorland villages beyond.

a certain point and to leave them 'at the crossroads on the road to Brendon'. Despite their claims of innocence, it was clear these tubs were part of the consignment that had recently been landed on Lynmouth beach.

The two labourers were obviously small pawns in the operation. Yet they were the ones who had been caught and they had to appear in court. They were convicted of smuggling, but their fines were immediately paid. Could the mysterious Appledore gentleman have provided the money to buy their silence?

13

The Last Years of Smuggling: 1833-1850

The smuggling run at Lynmouth in 1832 was one of the last major seizures on the Exmoor coast. At sea and on land the preventive forces were clamping down hard and the signs were that the illicit trade was gradually dwindling. Dying but not yet dead! In fact, smuggling would linger on for some years yet.

The Ilfracombe Customs collector seems to have been quite unaware that some contraband was still being run in on his section of coast. Several times he reported that the smugglers had deserted the region and no further seizures had been made. Yet in January 1834 the Customs Board wrote to him saying that information had been received that a small French vessel, *La Rosa* of Cherbourg, had successfully landed contraband on the coast somewhere near Lynmouth. Furthermore, the Board pointed out that on the following night the goods had been moved inland across the moor without being detected. Not a word of criticism appeared in the letter but the rebuke was there, nevertheless.

The following year saw the Porlock vessel *Prudence and Jane* being seized near Fowey in Cornwall. This was a reversal of the usual pattern of Cornish vessels being caught in the Bristol Channel, but whether the Porlock vessel was taking contraband from France to Cornwall, or collecting it in Cornwall to bring back to the Exmoor coast, it is impossible to tell.

Years passed without a single seizure. The preventive men may well have been lulled into a false sense of security, thinking the local smugglers had finally been vanquished, but one last flurry of activity was still to come. In July 1839 the principal Minehead Coastguard officer, accompanied by three Excise officers, found 220 tubs containing 683 gallons of brandy at Greenaleigh Farm, to the north-west of Minehead. Two years later Corporal Serpell, of the mounted Coastguard at Watchet, made two substantial seizures. The first, in April, was actually at the harbour and consisted of 123 tubs, containing 256 gallons of brandy and 127 gallons of gin, hidden in the Falmouth sloop *Kitty and Clara*. The second was of 173 tubs containing

32   The harbour at Porlock Weir in 1890.

528 gallons of spirits, which had been buried in the beach at Blue Anchor. The last recorded seizure in the region came in 1846 when 55 bales of tobacco stalks (used in the manufacture of snuff) were found on the shore at Ilfracombe. Presumably a contraband run had just taken place, but no one was caught and convicted.

By 1850 large-scale smuggling on the Exmoor coast had been virtually wiped out. The Government's new free-trade policy meant that import duties had been either slashed or entirely abolished and this had removed the incentive that for so long had driven the smugglers on. With the lure of fat profits gone, and faced with larger and better-organised preventive forces, the risks involved in smuggling no longer seemed acceptable. Here, as elsewhere on the British coast, the big operators gave up the unequal battle, leaving only a few petty traders to bring in a trickle of illicit goods.

Smuggling was coming to an end, but there were many good stories to tell. In his memoirs the Rev. William Thornton related how in the late 1840s duty-free liquor was still on sale on Exmoor to those who knew where to go looking for it. He said that it always tasted 'particularly choice', because a 'sense of irregularity added flavour to the dram'.

Outwardly respectable people were proud to have had some connection with the smugglers. The Rev. Thornton described how in the late 1840s he dined with a rector at Allerford, who told him that his cellar was stocked with excellent cognac and winked as if to imply it had been supplied by smugglers.

33   Glenthorne, c.1832. Smugglers often ran cargoes into the cove here because it was difficult for Revenue officers to properly police this remote stretch of coast.

The rector went on to explain how he came by it. One morning he had realised that two of his horses were missing. However, his coachman knew just where to look for them. They had been found in a lane beyond Exford. In their manger had been left a keg of brandy as a thank-you for the loan.

In 1853 William Thornton became curate of the parish of Countisbury and on one occasion had to minister to a dying smuggler. The old man revealed how things used to be done:

I sat by the deathbed of a very old smuggler, who told me how he used to have a donkey with a triangle on its back so rigged up to show three lanthorns and how chilled he would become as he lay out winter's night after winter's night, watching on the Foreland, or along Brandy Path, as we called it, for the three triangled lights of the schooner, which he knew was coming in to land her cargo where Glenthorne now stands and where there was a smuggler's cave. 'Lord bless you sir,' and the dying man of nearly ninety chuckled, 'we never used no water, we just put the brandy into a kettle and heated it and drinked it out of half-pint stoups, us did, and it never did us no harm whatsoever, it was of that quality it were.

The smugglers were passing on, but memories of them would live on in the Exmoor harbours and coves they had once frequented.

Glossary

Anker: a cask to hold wine or spirits, usually containing about 8 gallons.

Bohea tea: black China tea of the finest quality.

Brigantine: two-masted vessel with square-rigged foremast and fore-and-aft rigged mainmast.

Coastguard: the national preventive service established in 1822.

Coastwaiter: Customs official who supervised unloading of ships from British ports.

Collector: the principal Customs officer at a port.

Comptroller: the collector's deputy.

Cutter: a fore-and-aft rigged vessel, with one mast, two or more head-sails and a running bowsprit.

Excise: government office responsible for collecting duty on goods produced or sold within Britain.

Foresheet: inner part of the bows of a boat.

Galley: large open boat propelled by oarsmen.

Geneva: gin – in fact the word 'gin' is a modern abbreviation of geneva – mainly made in Holland and sometimes known as 'Hollands'.

Hogshead: a large cask: often held 52 ½ gallons.

Hovering: a vessel loitering off the coast waiting for an opportunity to run in contraband was said to be 'hovering'.

Land surveyor: Customs officer in charge of the officials who searched for contraband.

Landwaiter: Customs official who supervised unloading of ships from foreign ports.

Letter-books: in these books were kept copies of all letters sent and received by the collector.

Lugger: a small ship carrying two or three masts, each with a lugsail (a four-sided sail bent and hoisted on a yard).

Preventive Waterguard: came into being in 1810, had small rowing galleys and patrolled inshore waters.

Privateer: an armed, privately owned vessel holding a government commission to capture enemy merchant ships during a war.

Registry port: an official port, the collector kept a register of ships based there.

Riding officer: Customs officer who patrolled on horseback.

Rummage: a thorough search of a vessel by a Customs official.

Run: to import goods illegally.

Sea Fencibles: equivalent of a seaborne Home Guard set up during the Napoleonic Wars to guard against invasion.

Skiff: boat adapted for both rowing and sailing.

Sloop: a small one-masted fore-and-aft rigged vessel with mainsail and jib.

Tide surveyor: official who went out to vessels at anchor and rummaged their cargoes looking for contraband.

Tidesman: official stationed on board vessels in port to ensure no good were smuggled ashore.

Tub: a small wooden cask carrying only some 4 gallons, often favoured by smugglers as easy to carry.

Bibliography

Primary sources

Public Record Office
CUST 69   Customs Letter-Books, Barnstaple and Ilfracombe
CUST 70   Customs Letter-Books, Minehead
CUST 73   Customs Letter-Books, Swansea
T 1/352/41   Report of Commissioners for Customs on Memorial of
             Thomas Benson Requesting that Lundy be Established as a
             Place for Landing Ships (1753)
T 64/139   Report of William Culliforde on Frauds at Ports (1682)
T 64/145   Revenue Frauds, London and Western Ports (1723)

Newspapers
Exeter Flying Post
North Devon Journal

Secondary sources

Antony D.H. Coxe, *A Book about Smuggling in the West Country, 1770-1850* (1984).
Warren Derry, editor, *The Journals and Letters of Fanny Burney (Madame D'Arblay)* (1982), vol. 10.
Grahame Farr, *Ships and Harbours of Exmoor* (1970).
Grahame Farr, *'Smuggling Survey of North Devon'* (unpublished article and notes, 1970).
Alan G. Jamieson, *'Devon and Smuggling'* in Michael Duffy, *The New Maritime History of Devon* (1992), vol.1.
Lois Lamplugh, *Lundy: Island without Equal* (1993).
Frank McLynn, *Crime and Punishment in 18th Century England* (1989).
Geoffrey Morley, *The Government's Fight against Smuggling in the 18th and 19th Centuries* (1994).
David Phillipson, *Smuggling: A History, 1700-1970* (1973).
William Riddell, *Guide to Lynton and Lynmouth* (c.1885).
Graham Smith, *King's Cutters: The Revenue Service and the War against Smuggling* (1983).
Graham Smith, *Smuggling in the Bristol Channel, 1750-1850* (1989).
Suffolk Record Office (Ipswich Branch) S92, *'Memoirs and Travels of John Savage'* (1790).
Stanley Thomas, *The Nightingale Scandal* (1959).
William. H. Thornton, *Reminiscences and Reflections of an Old West-country Clergyman* (1899), vol. 2.
Mary Waugh, *Smuggling in Devon and Cornwall, 1750-1850* (1991).

Index